10 Steps to Breaking into Acting

2nd Edition

by

Matt Newton

WHAT OTHERS ARE SAYING ABOUT
10 STEPS TO BREAKING INTO ACTING

"Matt Newton is New York's smartest and most knowledgeable acting teacher and coach. His coaching and teaching come from a wealth of professional experience. He's a working actor, on-set coach for a hit television series and knows what those who hire need to see and hear from actors who are auditioning for them. And all of this he does with a keen eye and a kind heart."

-Brian O'Neill, author, "Acting as a Business"

"I wish I had this book when I started my career. Matt's knowledge of the business is remarkable."

-Becki Newton, actress

"Let me preface this review by saying that I have read countless numbers of books about breaking into the industry of TV and film. Matt has done something with this book that not only brings lots of insight, but does so honestly. If you are a beginning actor, serious about sharing your craft with the world through television and film, this book should be your Genesis. After reading it, I have such a greater understanding not only for the craft, but the business behind Hollywood productions! I'm very excited to see what the future holds!"

-Dan Checkley, actor

"This is a clear step by step guide to setting up your acting "business" as well as how to upkeep it at a professional level. It'll clear that foggy feeling of not knowing what to do next or even how to begin while being entertaining too! I'd definitely recommend buying it, reading it, re-reading it over and over to make sure you're hitting the right goals along the way! 5 stars."

-Nati Rabinowitz, actor

"I have referred to Matt's clear, concise and very personal writing in this book many times. It always brings me back to the "real" of acting. Matt has a natural way of sharing his experience and knowledge that is both grounding and inspiring. With Matt's advice and honesty I have found myself better able to get over the "initial" hang ups around acting and what it means. Even in Matt's 10 Steps to breaking into acting, his personality and truthfulness comes through, the same style in which he trains and teaches in person."

-Gerald von Stoddard, actor

"Not only is this book a fast and enjoyable read, it is packed with information. This is the type of book you want to keep handy so you can refer to every now and then. Matt Newton isn't preachy and he definitely doesn't brag about his own achievements (there are some embarrassing stories that are hilarious). He is concise, informative, and inspiring without pulling any punches. I highly recommend this book for anyone who wants a career as an actor."

-Nick Cornish, actor

"If you follow Matt Newton's practical advice when getting started, you'll avoid a lot of common mistakes and you'll be prepared to be your best in front of agents and casting directors. Matt writes honestly about how competitive this business is but he knows first-hand that when you're drawn to it -- you've got to go for it. This book will give you an edge. It's also full of very funny anecdotes about Matt's own path to being a successful actor -- and coach."

-Melissa Chamberlain, mom

"Mr. Newton's witty and concise book is an invaluable resource for any actor. While it is geared toward those aspiring to "make it" in this business, it is also particularly useful for those stage actors that may be pursuing a new direction doing commercials, films and TV. This book will help save you TIME, MONEY, and even perhaps a bit of your remaining sanity! Highly recommended."

-David Fox, actor

"I absolutely love this book! It is an incredible hands-on resource for everything you need to know as a beginner actor. The steps are simple, yet very useful, honest and essential if you want to break into acting. Matt, the author, talks from personal experience and you can definitely be sure that everything you read in *10 Steps to Breaking into Acting* is the truth. 5 stars, a must have!!"

– Mila Milosevic, actress

*This second edition is dedicated
to all of my wonderful students who inspire me every day*

Table of Contents

Foreword by Becki Newton 1

Introduction 4

Acknowledgements.. 8

My Story 9

STEP 1: Train, Train, Train...................................13

STEP 2: Type...20

STEP 3: Headshots...24

STEP 4: Resumé 30

STEP 5: Monologues..33

STEP 6: Finding Auditions 36

STEP 7: The Art of Auditioning..............................41

STEP 8: Demo Reels and Footage 57

STEP 9: Your Online Presence 61

STEP 10: Agents and Managers 64

Avoiding Scams...75

Survival Jobs..78

Kids and Teens 81

New York vs. Los Angeles....................................88

The Realities of Being on Set...............................92

10 Questions For a Casting Director.......................95

In Closing...97

Appendix A...100

Appendix B...101

About the Author 102

Foreword by Becki Newton

Playing Amanda on *Ugly Betty* was a once in a lifetime opportunity that involved an incredible amount of luck and timing. This was, in no uncertain terms, my "big break." But for actors just starting out, the more important question is: how did I go from a random girl arriving in NYC with a history degree and a dream of Broadway musical stardom to an actress working on TV? How did I get myself into the path of that opportunity?

Looking back, the series of "little" breaks in the very early stages of my career were far more instrumental in my current success than one single audition can encapsulate. I knew I wanted to be an actress, but had no idea how to start. I knew I had to be in New York City. Other than that, the one guide I had was my brother. He was one year ahead of me in the quest for becoming a professional actor. He had a year of mini successes and failures under his belt, and as a result, I was able to skip certain steps. He guided me directly to the agents I should call and the ones I should avoid. He even told me what time of day to call them. He referred me to exactly which headshot photographer to go to, after much trial and error of his own. His year of experience essentially provided me with a fast track and guidance that I couldn't have gotten anywhere else.

My early success came in commercials. I looked younger than my age and could somehow still pass as a teenager. My brother had been working with a commercial agent and one day I went with him to a *Colgate* audition. I did something you are definitely not supposed to do: I *crashed* it. I just walked right in and pretended I was supposed to be there. I just kept smiling as the casting director looked trough her submissions with a bewildered look on her face. Somehow I got a callback. And booked a role as an extra. My first paycheck as an actress!

From there, I continued to work in commercials. I loved them. I had so much fun auditioning--the more ridiculous the better. In many ways, commercial auditioning was my training for

1

my future comedic endeavors, in that I learned over and over how to NOT feel stupid. You need me to talk about how happy tampons make me while smiling into camera? No problem! You want me to sing about a board game while pretending to surf on a chair? Awesome!

Inevitably, my success in commercials led to television opportunities. I auditioned a million times for *Law and Order* and eventually got my first network TV credit: a quadriplegic rape victim. A guest star. My first little break. I literally crawled on the floor at the audition. After that, about three years after arriving in NYC, I got my first very *big* break. A series regular on a pilot. Contrary to popular belief, it was not for *Ugly Betty*. It was a show called *The Loop*. You may have seen it, and you probably won't remember me if you did, because I was recast when the show was picked up to series. It was a huge victory (I booked my first pilot!), followed by horribly ego crushing defeat ("we love the show but don't love you!"). I called my brother, who simply encouraged me to keep going. Back to commercials.

The week before I auditioned for *Ugly Betty*, I had filmed an *Olive Garden* commercial, playing a hostess who was way too excited about the breadsticks. It stayed on the air so long that later it even aired during commercial breaks of *Ugly Betty* years later (much to my *complete* horror). The day of my audition was a rough one. I had read for the lead role in *Men in Trees* (the role that Anne Heche definitely was already cast in) and got feedback afterward that I was "odd." Okay....? I walked into my *Ugly Betty* audition completely annoyed. I didn't particularly care if anyone liked me. I just wanted to get out of there. Apparently this attitude worked perfectly for what would turn out to be the laziest, most irritated, self-absorbed receptionist that ever graced the halls of Mode Magazine.

If my audition had been earlier in the day, before the icky phone call about how weird I was, my fate may have been much different. So much of it was timing, and I know how fortunate I am that the opportunity occurred in a moment in time where my attitude overlapped perfectly with a character I was trying to portray.

We don't truly know what audition will lead to a job that will "make" our careers. Any of them could. So it's best to be ready for success at all times. The truth is, without my brother's guidance about the business, I would never have known how to put myself in the path of success, and would never have broken in. Even if I had all the gumption in the world, I needed the basic tools and business organization to put my talent in front of people who could impact my career. So many elements of the business are out of our control as actors. No one can predict exactly how and when someone will come upon his or her "big break." However, certain people can help us along the way. I lucked out that I am related to one of these people. Thankfully, he is now helping so many others the way he helped me.

    -Becki Newton, actress (Ugly Betty, How I Met Your Mother)

Introduction

I wrote the first version of this book two years ago. At the time, more and more TV shows started filming in New York. It is now 2014, and there are currently over 30 TV shows filming in New York, a record number for this city. On top of that, Netflix, Amazon, Hulu, and even YouTube are now offering original content year round, offering tons of meaty roles for actors. Trends are rapidly changing, and I felt compelled to update my advice to make it as current as possible. Actors now have so many opportunities on both coasts, and if they are *smart*, they can find their niche in this business and begin a professional career as an actor.

An actor can now create his own webseries—write it, cast it, film it, put it online, and try to gather a following. Talent agencies are creating divisions specifically to look for actors who have a huge following on YouTube, in the hopes of parlaying that into a bankable career. At the same time, actors in New York and Los Angeles need to understand the *smartest* way to navigate the business of acting—Are pay to meet workshops worth it? What's the best way to approach an agent? Should I live in New York or Los Angeles? Should I pay to create my own demo reel?

I have been an actor for over 25 years (if you count bad dinner theatre) a professional TV and film actor for over 15 years (in both Los Angeles and New York), and an acting coach in New York City for the past 5. I would say I "broke in" to acting at age 23, when I booked my first speaking gig on a TV show (*Strangers with Candy*). I have been on thousands of auditions, coached thousands of actors (all over the world), and spent thousands of hours on film and TV sets, as both an actor and an acting coach. I've met and coached all kinds of interesting actors, some very successful (Emmy Award winners) and some just starting out. Young or old, they all had to start *somewhere*. Each one has an amazing, inspiring story of how they "broke in" to acting. For some, it's getting that first line on a TV show. For others, it's the first time they got recognized on the street, first time they walked on a student film set, or the first time they landed a supporting role in a big studio movie.

I get emails every day from actors all over the world, of different ages and backgrounds, asking me how to break into the business. What's the secret? Some want to be famous, some want to do it for fun, others want an escape, and others want to do it because they are hungry, driven, and ready to study the craft and deal with the rollercoaster of heartbreak and joy that comes with a career in the entertainment business. Some of them want a quick fix, like *"Oh, just call my agent and he'll help you out,"* or *"Why don't you stop by the set of 'Blue Bloods' and they will give you a speaking role,"* and some new actors want me to tell them if they "have what it takes." I wish it were that easy. If it were, I'd wave my magic wand and we'd have a lot more working actors than we do today. I've seen actors with no experience and no training go on to become extremely successful, and I've seen wonderful, talented actors who are amazing at their craft struggle for more than a decade to find an agent. Here are some emails I recently received.

> *"Hi Matt, what does a 44 year old do? I did 2 years of acting classes. I'm getting back into this now that I retired from the FDNY. I was also a cop. Both are great training grounds. I just think a coach would suit my needs. I'm older, more of a character type player. I just got new headshots. Not that crazy about them. I have updated my resumé. I'm in SAG. Where do I go now? LOL?"*
>
> -Tim, hopeful actor

> *"I would be interested in private classes for my 7 year old son. He has never had any coaching/training, but I believe he is talented, and I need an honest assessment and critique from a professional."*
>
> -Samantha, mom

> *"So, if actors don't have a degree from Yale, NYU, or Julliard, are we still able to make a career out of this?"*
>
> -John, actor

Mostly a lot of new actors just want *answers.* They are lost, uncertain, and need guidance. The business keeps changing, and actors have to keep up with the trends, educate themselves, avoid the scams, and learn the market. I wrote this book for these people, so they can get a better understanding of what it takes to break into the acting business in the two major markets: New York City and Los Angeles. I wanted to do this from a *working* actor's perspective, as someone who's *lived* it personally, who can relate to the journey, and who has since guided many others. I've spent several years helping actors break in and find lots of success, and for each actor, the path is different. I've learned that it's not enough to just be a good actor or a pretty face. You also have to be savvy. We have all these wonderful tools literally at our fingertips now, and new actors need to know how to navigate and learn the ropes in a smart and professional way.

When I first moved to New York, I made a lot of mistakes, went to mediocre headshot photographers, read the wrong books, almost fell prey to some scams, didn't even own a cell phone, and always wished I had someone telling me "Do this. Don't do this." I'm here to do that for you.

This is the book I wished I had when I started.

I wanted to give actors of all ages a practical, real, hands-on guide to get started in this business, and compete at a professional level. I like helping actors. Whether you want to do this professionally, or as a hobby, there are basic tools you must have as you begin to pursue this crazy roller coaster career. Here are the *essential* steps, the foundation. These are the tools that worked for me, and I hope they will help you on this amazing adventure you are about to embark on. Take this book with you. Keep it close. If you feel it would help somebody else, feel free to pass it along to them.

And do yourself a favor: remind yourself every day how lucky you are to be pursuing your dream. This is a wonderful, exciting business. I hope you enjoy every step of the journey.

Good luck!

Matt Newton, actor and acting coach

Acknowledgements

I have several important people to thank for their help in inspiring me to write the second edition of *10 Steps to Breaking into Acting*. First and foremost, I want to thank all of the wonderful actors who have read the first book, told their friends, took the advice to heart, and who have "broken in" to this business. Welcome to the club! I also have to give a shout out to all of my students, the amazing kids, teens, and adults that I work with every day. This book simply provides answers to the questions I've been asked by actors over the years, and without you, there would be no book at all. I thank you from the bottom of my heart for your continued inspiration, passion, intelligence, and diligence.

Other wonderful people who contributed, inspire me, and work their butts off are Carly Turro, Rosie Benton, Joseph Melendez, Nati Rabinowitz, Brian O'Neill, Pat Souney, the Terracianos, Matthew Blumm, Kimberly Graham, Mike Francis, Michael Kelly Boone, Christina Wright, Mia Cusumano, Marc Isaacman, Gil Choi, Laurianne Murphy, Tim Walsh, Leslie Zaslower, Dave Mckeown, Dani Diamond, Jeffrey Mosier, Dominic Coluccio, Rebecca Strassberg, Rachel Jett, and the *Blue Bloods* crew.

Finally, I want to thank the people closest to my heart. My mom, Jennifer, my sister Becki, my brother in law Chris Diamantopoulos, and my sweet wife, Liana Hayles Newton (who designed the cover). Oh, and I guess I should thank Bruce and Luna, my French bulldogs, who are currently scratching at my leg as I write this.

My Story

My first student film. I sucked. Seriously, I was so bad. I was a junior drama major at Vassar College, and this was my first foray into film acting. I was doing some major Shakespeare style "schmacting" in a very small frame, and my performance at best would have been described as "terrifying" or "embarrassing." It was my first exercise in "what *not* to do on screen." It was a short black and white piece of cinema where I played a frustrated film director, now on a dusty VHS tape in my closet at home in Connecticut, right next to my plastic, fake-brass drama festival trophies from high school, my signed *Guys and Dolls* cast poster, and my dusty, broken soccer trophies from middle school. Did *everyone* get a trophy?

I remember the night very clearly. I was so excited to go to the big film screening with all the *senior* film majors and drama students, who I worshipped. My hands were sweating, and I was nervous because I wanted everyone to think I was the next Matt Damon. The auditorium lights dimmed, the opening credits rolled, and then suddenly my big face popped up on the screen in all its overacting glory. I was mortified. Lesson learned. (Note to self: read Michael Caine's *Acting in* Film.) Let's call it a bump in the road, and a major reality check.

After that, I enrolled in more acting classes at school, auditioned for *all* the plays, got cast in some, rejected from many, and a week after graduation I decided to move to New York City. I loved acting, and I wanted to give this "professional actor" thing a shot. Acting was an outlet for me, my parents were supportive, and it gave me the happiness I was missing in other parts of my life. I liked being on stage, it brought me out of my shell, and I liked playing different characters. I was 22, I had a very expensive piece of paper with the words "B.A. Degree in Drama" in my hand, and I was ready to go.

Headshots, Survival Job, Apartment, Agent, Fame. That was my list. I wanted to break into acting, and I wasn't going to wait around for someone to give me permission. I knew I had to *make* people notice me, because it wasn't going to fall in my lap. I paid $200 for some pretty bad headshots (thought they were great at the time, even though I was wearing an old baseball hat in half of them and had bad razor burn on my neck). I immediately sent those out to fifty talent agents saying "I just graduated from Vassar College with a drama degree, I think I'm a good actor, you should sign me." Bad grammar, bad punctuation, the whole nine yards. I heard you should print your resumé on neon paper, as it really gets their attention. Nothing. No response. Lots of bad advice out there, folks.

I found an apartment in Long Island City with two "quirky" roommates, living above a Chinese restaurant. I went to bed and woke up smelling like pork-fried rice, probably because I ate it *all the time*. I bought the print edition of *Backstage* every Wednesday night at midnight at the subway newsstand in Queens, the *second* it came out (they didn't have an online site yet). I was cast as Paris in a production of *Romeo and Juliet* that a bunch of fellow drama majors were doing in a deserted parking lot on the Lower East Side (before that area was cool). We rehearsed every day, outside, in ninety degree heat. I remember one time we were rehearsing the scene where Romeo drinks the poison and some dude walked by and shouted, *"She ain't worth it, bro!"* I loved it. I was in the greatest city in the world, slowly inching my way forward. Crazies and all.

I walked into four temp agencies the day I moved to New York because I needed a survival job, and I knew I was good with computers (I could type seventy seven words per minute). I didn't wait tables because I had no experience, and thought that actually mattered (I guess you are supposed to lie). I bought the *Ross Reports* (now *The Call Sheet*) and sent my headshot to every casting director in New York *and* L.A., saying I would "fly myself to L.A." to be an extra on their show. Not kidding. Nobody had cell phones yet, so instead all actors had a $5/month answering service. I checked it ten times a day from my temp job, and thirty times at night from various pay phones around New York, hoping someone had called me to give me my big break. Nothing.

I spent every night of that hot summer locked in my pork fried rice sauna, dreaming of fame while mail-merging my form cover letter with my database of agent addresses (thanks temping!). I knew that snail mail takes one day in New York, so a day after I sent out headshots, I would call the agents listed on my Excel

10

spreadsheet and say, in my most eager voice: *"Hey, I'm Matt Newton, and I'm wondering if you got my headshot?"* Most of the time they hung up on me, and sometimes they said, *"We'll call you."* One time an agent said *"Hold on,"* took the time to find my headshot in their stack of hundreds, and said *"Sure, we'd like to have you come in for a meeting."* Wait...what? That really happens? Based on my bad headshot? Maybe they thought the razor burn was "edgy."

Suddenly I was "freelancing" with an agent, temping forty hours a week, performing *Romeo and Juliet* twelve hours a week in a parking lot, going to open calls on my lunch breaks, and reading *Backstage* cover to cover. But still I felt lost. When was I going to get paid and prove to my parents this was real? How would I get an agent? I read all the acting *business* books. Twice. None of the advice seemed to apply to *my* struggle. I technically had an agent, but quickly realized that didn't mean I would get auditions. I was non-union, had no demo reel, and only had high school and college theatre on my resumé. I was at the bottom.

Then I got on TV. The big time. Silver screen. Yup, I was an extra on an upcoming episode of *The Guiding Light.* I actually performed a Shakespeare monologue for the "Under 5" casting director to land that gig. I was well on my way to fame and fortune. I filmed it, and then a month later came home to Connecticut for the big viewing party with my parents, where everyone in town had heard that I was "the new guy" on *Guiding Light.* My parents had told everyone about it and--God bless them--they didn't know the difference between speaking roles and extra work. *Everyone* was watching that night. *"My son is famous!"* my mom told everyone who would listen—her hairstylist, co-workers, the plumber, and the entire extended Newton family. Well, that night we watched it, and in the middle of one of the bar scenes, right after a big reveal about the lead actress being pregnant with eight babies or something like that, my dad points to a blurry guy facing backwards in a bar scene with short, artfully spiky hair, and said *"That's you!"* I looked closer, squinted, and realized it wasn't me. They had cut me out of the show. Fail.

Time to step up my game. I needed training, or I was going to be an extra for the rest of my life. I took a four-week on-camera audition class with Marci Phillips, a wonderful casting director at

ABC (and author of the amazing book *The Present Actor*). She was honest, direct, and really opened my eyes to what I was doing wrong on-camera. She explained the casting process, how to stand out in auditions, what is expected, how to be confident and prepared. It was less about my acting *technique* and more about the *business* and mastering the art of auditioning. She told me my headshots weren't cutting it. I did my research and found an amazing headshot photographer that really captured my type and my personality. As a result of the training and the new headshots, I got more auditions, and more opportunities to move closer to my dream.

A couple of months passed, then one of the agents I was freelancing with *finally* got me an audition for a little independent film called *Newport South*. I barely had time to work on it, but I raced to the audition, changed out of my temping suit in the waiting room (Superman style), composed myself, artfully mussed up my hair, and went in and read for the casting director. I had sweat running down my face, and my L.A. Looks hair gel was losing its hold.

Long story short, the casting director thought I was great. I almost booked the movie, and he referred me to a manager, who *signed* me. That referral was gold. That manager then got me some meetings with some really big agents, and one of them "hip-pocketed" me. What's that mean? It means they were taking a chance on a totally undeveloped talent (with razor burn), based on a look and a referral from a big casting director. Then I booked my very first *speaking* role on TV, playing a blind football player on Comedy Central's *Strangers with Candy*. I felt like part of the club. I had "broken in." And then I moved to L.A. and stayed out there working in TV, film and commercials for eight years, before moving back to New York (I had a bicoastal agent, so it was an easy transition).

That is my story. It's different for everyone. You hear of people landing in L.A. and booking their very first audition, and you hear of people auditioning for ten or twenty years before they ever get paid as an actor. The bottom line is that you have to really want it, love it, and you have to have patience, talent, charisma, work ethic, and an unshakeable confidence in yourself.

STEP 1: Train, Train, Train

"Anyone can do that."

There is this misconception that it is easy to become an actor, and doesn't require much skill. We watch TV shows and movies and we think *"I can do that,"* or we hear about all these reality stars getting $200,000 an episode for playing themselves, or about an actor getting discovered at their high school, on the street, or in an elevator, etc. I'm here to tell you it isn't that easy, and that is the exception to the norm. So no more Googling "How to get famous," okay? A career in acting requires lots of patience, practice, resilience and knowledge, just like any other discipline. Yes, there are those rare actors that are born with talent, or "accidentally" fall into an acting career, but for most of us, our talent is hidden deep down, and we need to find someone to help bring it out, develop it, and nurture it.

Dancers train. Football players train. Boxers train. The best musicians practice every day. An actor must approach his career with the mindset and discipline of an athlete, and always be working to hone his craft, develop his technique, and improve his skills so that he is ready when a golden opportunity presents itself. Training is *essential.* It is the actor's safety net. It is what separates the good from the bad, the amateurs from the pros. On an actor's resumé, good training stands out. It shows how serious you are, especially when you have no credits to speak of...yet.

New York is the largest acting market next to Los Angeles. Chicago is a close third. There are actors coming out of Julliard, Yale, NYU, Carnegie Melon, and every other prestigious drama conservatory *every year* that are looking to get even *one* line on a TV show, or in a movie. There are over a hundred thousand actors in New York City, many more hopping off the plane every day in L.A., far fewer with agents, far fewer who actually get in the audition room, and far fewer who actually book the role. For a one line role on a hit TV show, a casting director could potentially get thousands of submissions from agents. It's a tough business, and unfortunately many people can't make a living as actors, and have to sustain themselves through survival jobs like waiting tables, temping, dog-walking, or anything else with flexible hours. Do you have to go to a conservatory? No. But you do have to know what you are doing. You *must* have some kind of solid acting technique to compete at this competitive, cutthroat level.

Sure, there are very successful actors out there who have never taken an acting class in their entire lives (Seth Rogen, Johnny Depp, Brad Pitt), but those are the exception. You are in one of the most competitive careers in the world, and you must be the consummate professional when you step into an agent interview, an audition room, onto the stage, or onto a set. You must have an aura about you that says, *"Trust me. I know what I'm doing!"* Even those actors you see on *Law and Order* who say *"He went that way!"* have probably had extensive theatrical training. Casting directors look for that. They love that!

To break into acting, you need to learn the essential tools, the foundation of acting technique. You also need to learn audition technique, and how to be "good in the room" as you will spend a lot of your career in the audition room, and it's a different beast altogether. You can't have one without the other. Actors need to learn how to develop a character, access every nuance of emotion, and use their body, voice, and imagination to make magic with whatever script is put in front of them. Without these skills, you will eventually fall on your face. To develop these skills, you need practice. When you get to New York or L.A., do yourself a favor, and find someone to train you and educate you on the craft and the business of acting. It can be life changing. There are many different types of teachers and classes, some better than others. Find someone who can bring out your best, be honest with you, who you connect with, who understands the business, and can prepare you for the road ahead.

There are *acting* classes and there are *audition* classes. An *acting* class will teach you about the basics of acting (objective, action, obstacle, conflict, character development, scene study, script analysis), and an *audition* class will teach you about the skill and etiquette of auditioning (cold-reading, acting on-camera, eye lines, connecting to the reader, the casting process, making strong choices, accessing emotions quickly, etc.). Both are important.

Acting Technique Classes

You need to learn how to control your voice, your body, your emotional range, and how to express yourself, whether it's in front a camera lens in an audition room with five people, on a film set in front of one hundred crew members, or on a stage in front of five hundred people. A good acting technique class can give you the tools for this, can challenge you, and help you bring out your original, interesting personality in your work. It can teach you how to analyze a script to find wonderful, interesting character choices. There are classes that meet once a week for several hours (good if you have a day job), and there are conservatories where you meet every day for three months (good if you have lots of excess money and time). These classes help you explore your strengths and weaknesses as an actor through exercises, scene study, script analysis, partnered work, and getting comfortable in front of a group. This is where you learn your craft, your approach, how to develop a character, how to discover your objective, your obstacle, your actions, and how to interpret a text to discover the subtext and feelings within. Find a technique that works for you, and allows you to be yourself while exploring all parts of your personality and emotional range. You need to know your limits as an actor before you can put yourself in front of the decision makers. A good technique will ground you in the scene.

Choose an Acting Technique

If you are pursuing a career as an actor, you probably know that there are many different techniques you can use to master your craft. Some of the better-known acting techniques are Sanford Meisner, Stella Adler, Stanislavsky, and Uta Hagen. These are the greats, and their techniques are taught by various disciples all over the country. Maybe one of these works better for you, or perhaps you want to find someone who teaches a combination of them. At the end of the day, it's about finding truth in your acting, and bringing your unique personality to your work. Actors should learn many different techniques, from many teachers over time. Find a class where you will get lots of personal attention, where you get up and work *every week*, with a teacher who *inspires* you, *motivates* you, *cares* about you, and is *honest* with you and your talent. It's your hard earned money. Use it wisely. If you can audit a class, do it. Group classes can be great because you are working with other actors, watching and learning from each other, and you can really learn to step out of your comfort zone and deal with things like nerves, stage fright, making mistakes, and feeling stupid in a safe, non-judgemental environment. The best classes will challenge you, allow you to make mistakes, and teach you the tricks of the trade and how to really be a strong, committed actor.

Decide on a Budget

Acting classes are an essential, necessary expense for actors. They are like headshots. You have to spend money to make money. Classes can range from $50 for one drop in class, $250 for a monthly class, $1000 for a 6 week class, or $10,000 for a semester long conservatory type environment. You pay for what you get. It all depends on the teacher's reputation, and what kind of environment you are looking for. I think actors should *always* be in a class of some sort, as it keeps you fresh, prepared and ready for when that next job comes along, whether it's next month or next year. If you are going to spend lots of money and go to someone just because they coached Reese Witherspoon eight years ago, just make sure you are going to be getting up to work in each class, and that you are getting personal attention and feedback. Some classes have twenty or thirty actors, and are very lecture focused, and some are small and allow the actors to get up and work all the time.

Audition Technique Classes and Workshops.

Let's say you have trained extensively and just need to brush up your audition skills. You are ready to get out there and get in front of casting directors. Find an *on-camera audition workshop* taught by someone who knows the business (a casting director, an on-camera teacher, or a working actor), treat it like a gym, and exercise your audition muscles every week so that you are ready when you get that first big TV or student film audition. Learn audition etiquette, where to look, how to command the frame, slate your name, connect to an off-camera reader, and bring a script to life. It's a different beast, and involves concentration and an active imagination. Spend your money wisely. Do your research, and make sure the teacher has legitimate credits and has real world experience, has spent time in auditions, on film sets, and understands the *business* side of acting. It is essential that all actors get experience in front of a camera when they are starting out. Make sure the class gives you a video of your scenes each week so you can really see what you are doing right or wrong, and rid yourself of any tics and bad habits you may have. On-camera acting is about relaxation, inner concentration, trusting the words, keeping your acting small and subtle (depending on the tone of the project), being natural, and learning to be still. It's about your eyes. You need to master the skill of on-camera acting and auditioning, and feel comfortable in front of the camera before you feel comfortable in high pressure TV and film auditions.

Commercial and Improv Training

Commercials can also be a great way to break in (as my sister did). Once you do enough commercials, TV and film casting directors start paying attention and you are more likely to cross over into the "legit" world. Even if you are young and beautiful, and all you want to do is be in commercials or on the latest CW show, you *still* must sharpen your on-camera skills so that you are prepared when you walk onto that set. If you just want to do commercials, improvisational training is a *must*. Most commercial casting directors bring in actors because they have strong improv training, as a commercial film shoot involves using that skill and bringing new life to very stale advertising copy. Casting directors want to see that you are adaptable, open, and can bring something new and different to the table. Look at the improv classes at the Groundlings, the Pit, or Upright Citizens Brigade. They offer monthly classes that teach you to think on your feet, activate your imagination, and think and feel "in the moment" without worrying about what you are going to say (an essential skill for commercial acting).

Don't be one of those actors who is too cool for acting classes. No matter how good you are, you have to learn how to create different characters, deliver lines with nuance, access emotions quickly, take direction on the fly, calibrate your acting for the camera, be natural and conversational, relaxed, focused, bring a sense of spontaneity, hit your mark, "save it for the close-up," and develop a sense of confidence that good training provides.

Private Acting Coaches

Maybe you are new to the business, want to get your feet wet, have never been on a stage before, and you are shy in front of people and scared of taking a class. Private coaches can be great for newer actors, because you can sign up for one hour sessions devoted entirely to you, with no distractions, with an amazing teacher, and you can develop and learn very quickly, whether you are interested in TV, film or theater, need help with auditions, monologues, business strategy, or want to start from the very beginning. Prepare to spend more money for this. A good acting coach will be honest with you, zero in on your strengths and weaknesses, and give you new skills in a short amount of time. It is intense, *focused* training. There are coaches that work on acting technique, character development, camera training, finding monologues, and there are coaches that will help you when you get that big audition for Martin Scorsese. Other coaches can coach you on business strategy, your type, and targeting agents. A good coach can be a mentor, a friend, hold you accountable from week to week, and can guide you through the rest of your career and bring you to the next level. You want someone that will *challenge* you, *push* you out of your comfort zone, and give you *honest* feedback. Most importantly, you have to vibe with them and love their approach. If you don't live in New York or Los Angeles, many coaches offer you the ability to do Skype sessions with them, which can be a wonderful way to learn if you don't live in a major market.

How to Find a Good Acting Teacher

Hands down the best way to find a good class or acting coach is through referrals. Ask your friends, check out *ActorRated*, *Backstage* message boards, forums, read reviews, and see what other actors are saying, and the experiences they had. A good Google search will do wonders. Decide what your budget is, call around, look at websites, and ask if they offer a free consultation or audit first. The most important thing is that you *connect* to the teacher, and that they understand you and what you are looking to achieve. Do their clients get work? Do you relate to their approach? Do you like their technique? Are they supportive but honest?

You want to continuously develop your acting technique, so that when you do "break in," and get your first role, you are ready. Even well known actors continue to train. The famous director David Fincher (*Social Network, Zodiac, Fight Club, Gone Girl*) is notorious for making his actors do dozens and dozens of takes for each shot (sometimes even fifty takes!). Let's say you have a scene where you have to cry. Are you able to do it fifty consecutive times? That's a lot of menthol. If you were in a Broadway show, can you recreate that big emotional scene eight times a week? Probably not. That's where a good technique comes in. Natural talent will only get you so far. At some point you are going to have to broaden your range and expand your skills, or otherwise you are going to be a one-trick pony.

Practice, Practice, Practice

At the end of the day, actors need to always be training so that they are ready when that wonderful opportunity comes along. Take a class, work with a coach, get involved in anything and everything in your town. It can change your life and jumpstart your career. Download scenes from TV shows and tape yourself reading them with a friend, practice memorizing monologues, get involved in community theater, student films, be an intern in a casting office, a reader for a casting director, write, produce your own webseries, do whatever you can to keep that muscle strong.

STEP 2: Type

There was this acting class I heard about in L.A., where on the first day, before anyone said anything, each actor would take turns going up in front of the class. Then everyone in the class would shout out the first "type" that came to mind. HOOKER! FRAT GUY! DRUGGIE! SEDUCTRESS! FUNNY CHUBBY GIRL! YOUNG DAD! OLD HIPPIE! HOTTIE INGENUE! WEIRDO CREEPY LADY! OTHER WORLDLY PERSON! It's harsh, but it's the most eye-opening acting exercise (and sometimes shocking). We might think we are one thing, but people may perceive us very differently. Everything from our hairstyle to our clothes to our weight matters. It's one of the first things I discuss when new clients come to me who want to break into acting:

What is Your Type?

It's the single most important question in acting, and one that I wish I had figured out sooner rather than later. Obviously you need great headshots, a resumé, a demo reel, and a good business sense. But before that, you have to know how people *perceive* you, and where you *fit* in to this business. Your niche. It is a business, after all, and it's all about how you market yourself.

When I graduated college, I thought I could play any type. I thought I was sooooo good, that I could play parts twice my age, half my age, I even played a female character once in a play (experimental theatre at its finest). My very first real audition post college was for a sixteen year old contract player on *As The World Turns.* I was twenty three years old, and I was in the waiting room with high school kids and their parents. Nobody ever said to me "You look young, Matt. You will be auditioning for high school students for a couple of years." I wore my favorite oversized high school prom blazer with shoulder pads, a loose v-neck, and pleated khaki pants to that audition. No callback.

With TV and film, it's a *marketplace.* What are the types that are making money? You need to put yourself in the audience's shoes, in the casting director's shoes. Are you a young handsome leading man or an older quirky character actor? Which

20

types are cast over and over again in commercials and on your favorite TV shows? The funny chubby sidekick or the stoner best friend? The hot ditzy blonde girl or the haggard junkie? Here are some other types: newbie lawyer, young mom, cool hipster artist, blue collar guy, quirky nerd, thug, frat guy, bimbo, funny best friend, bad-boy, wise-ass, bully, slick salesman, etc. There are tons. It's not what you *are,* it's what you *play.* My sister is one of the nicest people you'll ever meet. Yet she played the mean assistant on *Ugly Betty* for four years!

When you walk into a room, your type is the first thing that pops into an agent or casting director's mind. After all, the audition starts the moment you walk in the door. They are already assessing and making decisions. Not good-looking enough, not tall enough, not confident enough, not scary enough, too macho, too "soft," etc. It is TV and film after all. Play the game, know it's a business, and don't take it personally if you are thought of a certain way, or if you only get called in for serial killer roles. And when I say that, I mean *own* who you are. *Don't* change your personality. *Don't* get plastic surgery. *Don't* try to be somebody else. There's nothing more attractive than someone who is comfortable and confident with himself. You are constantly going to be making first impressions on people. Find what makes you unique (your curly hair, your biting humor, your quick wit, your weight, your freckles, your tattoos), and show it.

Michael Kelly Boone, a talent agent at Leading Artists Agency in New York, puts it like this: *"Take a good and honest look at yourself in the mirror. In TV and film, that's what you're going to play. Know who and what you are. Leave the 'acting' for the stage."* You can be the smartest person in the world, and still go out for the "dumb jock." You might not even play sports! Are you the young leading man who could play the new love interest on *Flash* or are you the creepy old villain on *Homeland?* Does your face say *Teen Wolf,* or does it say *Walking Dead?* Are you the smart, clean cut and sophisticated young lawyer, or the early thirties slacker type? Don't let this assessment put you off. Later in your career you can start branching out from your type, once you start booking *lots and lots* of work.

3 Ways to Nail Down Your Type

Let's get honest. While it's easy to look at others and get a sense of their natural type, doing the same for own your self can be daunting. Where do you even start? Here are some easy steps to nailing down your type.

Write down three actors who are stealing jobs from you. I mean, watch TV, look on IMDb-Pro, go see movies, and find out which actors are playing parts that you were *meant* to play. Age, ethnicity, looks, personality, everything. That's where your journey begins. What is unique about them, and why are they being cast in these roles? It's about talent. But they have also cornered their market on that type. What else have they done? Have they always played this type? Some headshot photographers will talk to you about this before they shoot with you so that they can help you present yourself the right way.

Write down three shows you could see yourself on. Series regular, guest star, costar...whatever. There are over thirty shows filming in New York right now, over one hundred in Los Angeles. Watch them, learn from them, observe what kind of actors they are casting. Take notes. Look up the casting director and the actors. If you are right for that show, and are trained, and they cast your type over and over, then by all means sign up for a casting director workshop to meet them in person. If you are over fifty and play "extraterrestrial" roles all the time, it's probably not wise to sign up for a soap opera casting director workshop. Again, it's all about being smart and knowing yourself.

Finally, ask your close friends, an acting coach, or anyone who will be honest with you. Your good friends will be honest with you. Coaches will be honest. Your mom won't. In my classes, type identification is an important discussion. Each person sits in the front of the class, while everyone else anonymously writes down their different opinions on that actor's type on one notecard, and passes it around. At the end of the class, that actor gets that notecard, and on it are a bunch adjectives and opinions on their type. It's very eye opening, very honest, and is an essential tool to presenting yourself the right way in this business. After all, it's exactly what casting directors are thinking from the moment you walk into the room. It should be reflected in your headshots, your audition monologues, your demo reel, your attitude, your personality, the way you carry yourself, your brand, and ultimately strongly impacts your marketability.

Know who you are and own it. It's the single most important piece of advice I'll ever give you. I spent years trying to figure it out, and always trying to be what *they* wanted. Instead of just being myself. My quirky, All-American, boy-next-door self. Not quite leading man, not quite the sidekick. The better grasp you have of yourself, the easier your career will be.

STEP 3: Headshots

"My friend took my headshots."

Now that you know your type, and you found a great coach or teacher, it's time to get *headshots*. Your first marketing tool. No iPhone pics, no Instagram pics, no glam-style JC Penny shots with a paradise backdrop and your chin resting elegantly on your hand. You can't audition without headshots.

My first headshot session was rough. I wore a baseball hat in all the shots, the pictures were bad, the photographer was eighty five years old and out of touch with the marketplace, and I looked bad in them. I didn't know my type, I had a sucky haircut (a "suck-cut" as my sister calls it), my shirt was two sizes too big, and I had razor bumps all over my neck (just started shaving). Jealous?

I can't tell you how many people come to me and say "I have some headshots that my friend took last week on his point and shoot." More like point and *sh*t* (oh, snap!). Ninety percent of the time they are horrible, and would best be suited for a Facebook pic (or better yet, Myspace). Ten percent of the time they might work on your grandmother's piano, or on her mantle next to your awkward middle school portrait.

Headshot (noun): a state of the art, badass, professional 8x10 pic that is full of personality and will get you noticed.

It's your *calling card* (*"Call* me in for an audition!"), your introduction to the marketplace, so treat it as such, and present yourself as professionally and honestly as possible. Would you wear ripped jeans to a job interview? Then don't bring an amateur headshot to an audition! It shows you don't care and that you don't take yourself and your career seriously. It's your foot in the door (or your head), your chance to show people your personality, your professionalism, and that you are ready to play at a competitive level. Most casting director's receive only digital submissions from agents now, so the little JPEG of your headshot becomes even more important than ever before (the color, the brightness, the clothing). Gone are the days of casting directors sifting through hundreds of 8x10's on their desk. The picture has to stand out in a *"I want to hire that actor"* way, not in a *"That person really scares me"* way. Don't skimp, don't have your friend do it (*please*), and don't shortchange yourself.

7 Tips for a Better Headshot

Here is what you need to keep in mind when it comes to your headshots.

Go pro. Spend the money. It's worth it. Go to a professional, who is trained, understands lighting, and takes headshots for a *living*, not some friend who happens to have a decent camera who "sorta knows a little about photography." Save those pictures for Instagram, and leave the headshots to the pros. Good headshots range from $400-$1200, and to get them professionally duplicated (not at CVS) will cost you another $100. Anything less is just a glorified passport photo. If the headshots look cheap, they probably are. And you look like you don't care about your career.

Go for personality over glamour. Make sure it looks like you. Chill with the airbrushing. Casting directors expect you to look just like your headshot, and will not be happy when you show up looking totally different, or ten years older. It's not about looking pretty, it's about representing your *type,* wrinkles and freckles included. It should look like you on your best day, showing your age, and who you are *now.* It's not about the type you *want* to be, it's the type you *are.*

It's all about the eyes. Just like with on-camera acting, it's all about the eyes, and what's happening behind them. It's your close-up, your moment. Your eyes should be perfectly in focus, alive, and energized, and not dead and glazed over. There should be strong inner thoughts, implying a backstory and a life behind the eyes. A slight squint, and strong piercing eyes will bring a picture to life and help it stand out in a pile of hundreds. A good headshot photographer knows how to bring this out in you. The eyes should be crisp.

Pay attention to framing, lighting, and background. In general, a good headshot is chest up with good lighting on your face, and no strong dramatic shadows, unless you are going in for

The Phantom of the Opera. Three-quarter shots are good for print, and extreme close-ups are good for, well, nothing. Look directly into camera, and the focus should be on the center of your eyes, not your left ear, or your shirt collar. No peace signs, weird facial hair, or the famous "hand on face" pose. Be sure the background is blurred, which means it's shot with a good, high quality camera with a high-depth of field, which makes you stand out. We don't need to see that you are standing on the beach in Santa Monica, or on a tour boat in front of the Statue of Liberty. It's about you, not the environment.

Natural light vs. studio. Some photographers do both, as they offer a different look and feel. Natural light gives a very real, "film" look, which I prefer. Studio lighting tends to be a little more polished, with a more neutral backdrop. Both can be wonderful. If you are more of a sitcom or commercial actor, perhaps a good well-lit studio headshot is more suited for you. If you want to look like you are on *True Detective*, then go for the outdoor look.

Clothing and props. I once saw a headshot of a guy with a bird on his head. Why? Because he wanted to stand out. Let's not get crazy here. Keep it simple and classy, and follow the standard format. Professionalism gets you noticed, not desperation or gimmicks. Leave the Ed Hardy and the "statement" shirts at home. A simple, solid color shirt with a little texture that fits you well and matches your eyes should do the trick. No whites, and no graphics or anything you think might distract from your face. And no props. (You know that, right?) If you think you are going to play cop roles, you don't need to wear the outfit in the headshot.

Don't go crazy with the makeup. Yes, lots can be done with retouching. There is no need to put on tons of makeup, or pay hundreds to have a "makeup artist" at your shoot. You want to look like yourself on your best day, and not look like you tried too hard. Girls--be yourself, do your hair the way you would for every audition. Guys--bring some oil sheets to take down the shine, and maybe use a lightly tinted moisturizer to take out the redness and even your skin tone. Some people spend way too much on makeup, only to have to get their headshots redone afterwards because they look fake in all of the photos.

Choosing the Photographer

Do your research and find the best photographer you can that is also within your budget. Expect to spend at least $400 on headshots (some charge $1200) for a two look package (change of clothes, with facial hair and without, hair up and hair down), with a full online proof sheet. Then you will pay another $100 to have fifty 8x10 hard copies of your favorite pic (or two) made that you will bring with you to auditions, mail to agents, hand to Stephen Spielberg in the elevator, etc. Yes, it will cost you money. But in this business, you need to spend money to make money. A great headshot is *essential.*

Find a headshot photographer who will give you different looks, indoor and outdoor, close-up and medium shots, with different expressions, different lighting, and will show different sides of your personality. You should look at as many portfolios as you can online, find photographers within your budget who take pictures of people *like* you. Do they specialize in children? Older people? Are their pictures young and hip? Do they do both indoor and outdoor shots? How many looks do they do? Do they give you retouched images? Do the pictures look cheesy and forced, or natural and timeless? Do they understand the current trends? Are you more comfortable working with a man or a woman? You should *love* their pictures. You should go to someone who has an extensive portfolio, who understands actors, who has studied lighting and photography, works with great equipment, and who really knows how to make you feel relaxed and bring out your personality in the shoot. Ask for referrals, look at your friends' headshots, look online, meet with photographers in person, etc. Getting headshots taken is awkward, so if you are going to spend your well-earned money on them, you have to feel comfortable with the photographer, because these will last you for years.

Jeffrey Mosier, a prominent headshot photographer in New York, says:

> *"When you see a headshot, can you visualize yourself in a similar setting with the same type of look? Do you know actors that a certain photographer has shot with? Did they capture the*

essence of that person? YOU need to come through in the shots more than anyone can possibly stress. There are a ton of pretty pictures to be had out there, but it is my belief that a headshot should go way beyond that. You want to grab a casting directors attention and then make sure they have no option but to call you in. Headshots are not about cameras or fancy lighting, it's all about what you have to say. Capturing that should be a collaboration. Make sure you jive with your photographer!!"

Choosing the Headshot

Once the session is done, the photographer will send you an online proof sheet of all the shots, and you have to go through and *pick* your headshot. This is the hard part. Make sure the pictures you choose resemble your *type*. First impressions matter, and this picture will be passed over very quickly on a casting director's computer screen or desk. It has to *pop*. Don't post it on Facebook and pick a headshot based on the amount of "likes" you get. Bad move. Ask a few people whose opinion you trust and maybe who don't know you that well, and narrow it down to three that show different sides of you (one for commercial, one for film and TV, and one backup.

Now take that high-resolution image on a CD to a *headshot reproduction* house. (My favorites are Colorworks and Reproductions). If you need mild retouching, they can do it for you for a low fee (some photographers include this in the price). Again, keep it simple with the retouching. If you have moles all over your face, keep them in. If you have a lazy eye, well...*embrace* the lazy eye. Retouching is for minor issues like smoothing out the redness in the face or taking out the eye puffiness and dark circles from that bender the night before.

When you show up at an audition, you should look *exactly* **like your headshot.** If you are way prettier in your headshot than you are in person, you will make the casting director mad and they won't bring you back. If you are a big guy, don't try to hide that in your picture by not showing your body. Again, this is all about knowing your type and owning it. Just because it's a beautiful picture of you doesn't mean it should be your headshot. What image are you conveying? How will you be cast? Be realistic when choosing which headshot you are going to use. It's about your brand.

This is the picture you will be sliding under Martin Scorsese's door. Do you really want to give him that creepy pic of you that your friend took in front of the Central Park statue that makes you look like a criminal, or that amazing *professional headshot* that you paid good money for that makes you look like a serious actor?

STEP 4: Resumé

"I was in the ensemble of 'Grease' in high school." So was I.

Your RESUMÉ. That manifesto stapled to the back of your headshot. That piece of paper that shows all of the amazing things you have done. Along with your picture, this is the single most important marketing tool you have as an actor. A resumé says *"I've worked! I know what's like to be on a set. I know how to create a character. I've taken tons of classes and I'm ready to step up to the next level."* It is an essential piece of the puzzle, and one that will hopefully always be changing as you get closer to breaking in.

Your resumé should include your name, cell phone, email, union status, website (if you have one), followed by the categories (Theatre, Film, TV, Training, Skills). Do you know how many people leave out their contact info? No crazy font, no made up credits. Just the facts, ma'am. If you are new and starting out, put anything and everything you've ever done on there. One credit is better than no credits, even if it was just a church group performance of *South Pacific* in your backyard. Seriously. Everyone has to start somewhere, and as you gain more credits, you will slowly chip off the ones that seem small.

Headshot and resumé go hand in hand. On the other side of an 8x10 photo is an 8x10 resumé, printed and stapled on the back. Print your resumé out on white copy paper and cut it down to 8x10 so it fits on the back of your headshot (not with scissors, go to Kinko's and use their fancy paper cutter). That is the *industry standard*. You don't need fancy paper here. Save your money. This is different than going in for a computer-consulting job. All that matters is what's on there, and what you look like. (See Appendix B for a sample layout of a resumé.)

If you have an out of state cell phone number, change it to a New York number. If you have a weird email address (imgonnabeastarr@hotmail.com), change it to a more professional one (ideally one associated with your website, such as matt@mattnewton.com). Immediately. Present yourself like a professional, and you will be treated as such. There are far too many amateurs out there.

30

Listing Your Credits

If you were an anchor for your high school news station, put it on here. If you did an anti-drug PSA for your public access station in your hometown, put it on there. If you were in a middle school production of an original musical about sausages, put it on there. Community theatre, church theatre, readings, camp productions, industrial films, whatever. It shows that you have been on stage and have experience as an actor, even if you were performing on cafeteria tables in your eighth grade lunchroom (where I did *my* first show). Even if the shows were over forty years ago, and you are returning to acting after a big break. Other industry people will disagree with this statement, but in my experience it's far better to show them that you've worked. You will slowly wean out the smaller credits as you go along.

Don't worry if you don't have a lot of credits on your resumé. Ideally your amazing headshot and training will help you get auditions at the beginning. And don't *ever* pad your resumé with fake credits. Trust me, someone will call you out on it.

Skills

You must be good at something, right? It's really a category about "conversation pieces," or if you do anything cool, like speak a foreign language fluently (many shows and commercials need this!), or are an expert in shot put. If you have nothing, put a bunch of sports down on there that you've played, or if you sing and play guitar. Please tell me you are good at *something.*

Extra Work

Here's a little note about Extra Work (or "background" or "atmosphere talent"). *One* day is all you need to see what it's like on a set. A lot of new actors do it many times, get their union waivers, and a lot of them think it's okay to put on the resumé. It's great to see what it's like on a big film and TV set and learn the lingo, but *don't* put it on your resumé. It's not acting, and when you put it on your resumé, it screams *"I'm an amateur and I love not speaking on TV!"* As you read in the beginning, I did one day of extra work in my life, and although it was a great experience, I knew that I *never* wanted to do it again. I loved seeing all the cameras, the lights, and being close to the stars and watching them act. It opened my eyes to this world, and I sat there for ten hours thinking *"I wish I was the one talking."* Some people do it for years, and make decent money being union background artists. It's just not for me. I'd rather wait tables.

When you get caught in that world of extra work, there's a real feeling of "It's so near, but yet so far" every time you are on set. People just don't get discovered being extras on shows. Sure, I know actors that have been given a line or two at the last minute, but it's not common, and you should never go into it expecting that. Central Casting is the big extras agency in New York that will connect you to doing extra work on big TV shows and movies, if that's your wish.

STEP 5: Monologues

Now you are ready to audition, to books jobs and boost your resumé. You are ready to go to battle, to fight the good fight, and deal with lots of rejection. But before that, you need something to audition *with*. Your resumé is blank, you have no demo reel, why would anyone hire you? You need to show them you are *good*. This is where your monologues come into play.

Monologue (noun): An amazing, kickass, fully memorized, one to two minute speech that shows how talented you are. You need at least one comedic monologue, and one dramatic monologue.

Why You Need Monologues

When you are first starting out, some casting directors and agents ask for a monologue to assess your talent, especially at the controversial "pay to meet" showcases (more on that later). It shows them your personality, and gives them a snapshot of your technique and command of character and language in a short amount of time. When you get to the point where you are working with an agent, you really won't need them as much, because at that stage in your career people already trust that you are good, and you will always be reading a scene from the script (also called "sides") for their project. But for now, monologues are crucial.

When I meet with new clients, after we discuss type, I get them working on their monologues *immediately*. And guess what? They always thank me later. Because when you are up for a role, or when you get a meeting with an agent, they just *might* ask you to perform two contrasting monologues for them (that's what happened to me in my first agent meeting). You don't want to be the actor that says "*Uh, I don't really have one.*" Consider that opportunity missed. You always have to be ready. Monologues, demo reel, everything.

What Makes a Good Monologue

Like your headshot, your monologues should reflect your *type* and your *age,* but they should not be monologues people have heard a million times (*"To be or not to be..."*). You want to be original, and give a casting director or agent a brief snapshot of your talent and your personality. This is the YouTube generation, and everyone has a short attention span, after all. Nobody wants to see a five minute memory monologue (*"I remember when I was growing up on that farm in Kansas..."*), and nobody wants a "shock" monologue (*"F#$k you s#@#$@#my sorry m*thaf!@er!,"*). Keep it short, simple, and honest. Casting directors and agents make up their mind within the first fifteen to thirty seconds, so it really has to be effective in grabbing their attention.

A good monologue is one where your character is *urgently* going after something that he or she needs *right now.* It's active and alive, powerful and conversational, modern, involves another imaginary person, and engages the listener quickly and effectively. It has a beginning, a middle, and an end, and we watch the character go through this journey in the course of one to two minutes.

You should be able to present this monologue at any given moment, in any situation, when you are asked for it. And you *nail* it every time, and are fully memorized. I personally think you should have at least four contrasting monologues that show your type and your age (two for TV and film, and two for theatre).

How to Find a Monologue

The lesser known, the better. The best place to find a monologue is from an obscure play, TV show, or indie movie. Something not many people have heard before. You can also find a selection of plays in the Drama section of Barnes and Noble or your local bookstore (or better yet The Drama Bookshop in NYC). A better move would be to find a part from a play where you can piece together a monologue by cutting out the other character's lines. Google "overdone monologues" and you will find which ones *not* to do.

Internet and Monologue Books

Please don't watch YouTube videos and copy some random actor in Texas doing his best Laurence Olivier impression. You laugh, but new actors do it *all the time*. You can find monologues on the internet or in monologue books, but I'm telling you right now, they are probably overdone (and done badly). If a monologue is that easy to find, then that means that many other people are finding it too (because they are lazy). Your goal is to be original and interesting, and you don't want to be copying what other actors are doing. You have to *love* these monologues, relate to the characters, and read the plays that the monologues are from so that you understand the context. You have to constantly be obsessing about ways to make yourself stand out. Find something that fits your type that nobody has seen before, and work with a coach to connect to the material and really make it really stand out.

Presenting a Monologue

It's about creating images out of thin air, and really feeling like someone is there listening to you and reacting to you. Ground yourself, breathe, and let the speech unfold from moment to moment, while reacting to nonverbal responses from another human imaginary human being standing in front of you. Never look directly at the casting director, as it makes them uncomfortable, and they want to watch you and take notes without feeling like they are being put on the spot and *forced* to look back at you. Only when you are reading sides from a script do you ever look at the casting director, as they will usually be reading with you, and are looking for that eye contact and that connection.

This is your business, and you are the product, and you have to treat is as such. You want to show people how serious you are. Give them something they haven't seen before, and knock it out of the water. In a sea of thousands of actors, you want your monologue to stand out just as much as your headshot.

STEP 6: Finding Auditions

Now you are ready for the fun part. Finding auditions. You are ready to go out into the world and show them what you got. You were born to do this. Your monologues are polished and ready to go, your headshot and resumé are formatted correctly, your on-camera acting and audition skills are solid, and you are chomping at the bit. But here's the deal: because you don't have an agent, you won't have access to the big TV and studio films that are casting. For now you have to start smaller. You are looking at non-union films, specs, readings, music videos, short films, and industrials.

Breakdowns

Breakdowns are brief descriptions of the different roles for a project and what they are looking for in terms of type (i.e. "male, late twenties, Caucasian"). When you have an agent, those big breakdowns for film, TV and theatre projects are sent out through a company called *Breakdowns Express* directly from major casting directors to agents and managers, so they can submit their clients, and so random actors all over the world aren't sending in thousands of headshots for every one line costar role on *Blue Bloods*. Yes, there are actors who pirate breakdowns illegally, but I promise you that it doesn't help you in any way, except remind you of all of the jobs you are missing. Until you are one of the lucky elite to have *theatrical* representation (i.e. TV, film, theatre) or *commercial* representation, you have to work your way up. This business is about relationships. Casting directors have *relationships* with agents and managers, and trust they will submit highly qualified actors for each speaking role. If they opened up the submissions to anyone and everyone, it would take forever for casting directors to sift through the most qualified actors. This is why agents and managers exist in the first place. It makes the casting director's job that much easier. So your mission is to work your way up so that agents see you as a well groomed professional who is ready to be submitted for network TV shows.

Online Casting Sites

To get auditions, you have to comb the trades and the reputable online audition sites to find projects that are looking for your type. In L.A., the reputable sites are Actors Access, Casting Networks (called LA Casting), and *Backstage*. In New York, the best online audition sites are *Backstage*, Mandy, Actors Access, and Casting Networks (called NY Casting). There are other ones, but these are the best. To be part of these, you have to subscribe. Most of them charge a small monthly or yearly fee, except for Mandy. When I started, *Backstage* was my bible. Because I didn't have an agent, this was the only place to find out about all the auditions that were happening in New York City.

Because you are not in the union yet, you will be looking at "non-union" gigs. Non-union is anything and everything that any person with a camera and a dream wants to create. Anything that is *not* SAG-AFTRA (the recently merged actor's union). Basically it's copy-credit-meal gigs, which means you might get an IMDb credit, a nice meal (or crackers), and most importantly great footage, which will help you build an amazing demo reel, which you will put on your website, which will get you an agent. Get it? More on that later. You will be submitting to music videos, student films, plays, open calls, readings, short films, feature films, webseries, TV spec pilots, extra work (hopefully not), etc. You have to make sacrifices to work your way up, and sometimes that means taking a day off work to shoot a student film for free, and waiting six months to get the footage.

Once you sign up for a reputable audition website (a nominal yearly fee), you can post your headshot and resumé (and demo reel if you have one--more on that later), and immediately start submitting for jobs that are right for you. The casting notice will tell you where to email your headshot and resumé (some will let you submit right through your smartphone!), when the auditions are, and what *types* they are looking for (there's that word again). Go through it, see if they are casting your type somewhere, and send in or email your headshot and resumé with a brief note that says "Please consider me for the role of...." Then pray that they call you for an audition.

I suggest signing up for at least two sites. There will be some overlap with projects, but at least you have your bases covered. You can bookmark them on your computer, your phone, your "phablet," and have casting notices sent to you as soon as they are posted. Boom! Submit. There's nothing more exciting than seeing a breakdown that fits you perfectly! The sooner you submit, the better, as that casting director is getting hundreds if not thousands of submissions from actors just like yourself.

So you figured out your type, and you know you're a good looking Caucasian guy in your early to mid twenties, and there's a role in a New York Film Academy student film that's perfect for you. Great. Submit yourself. There's also a one-day shoot on a new web series, any ethnicity, age twenty to forty, no pay, copy provided. Great. Submit. Every day new auditions are being added, so you should obsessively be checking these sites and combing through them in real time.

A lot of projects are cast from self-tape now, and some auditions are even done through Skype. Learn to be a master of self-taping and proficient in Skype. Trust me, many people don't have a clue. You can now submit from anywhere. Let It Cast is a great international submission site. A casting director might put out a breakdown for actors through Facebook or Twitter, and ask them to self-tape their audition and email it. Casting directors used to fly all over the country to scout talent. Now it's as simple as an actor uploading a self made video and hitting "send." Good HD cameras are very affordable now, so every actor should have one, and know how to professionally self-tape their auditions.

Craigslist

Don't search for auditions through Craigslist. Most of the time they are sketchy. Sometimes they are not. I know it's free and all, but any respectable director or casting director will pay the small fee to post their casting on a real site, geared towards serious actors. Always look up producers and directors on IMDb-Pro to see if they have verifiable credits. I've heard too many stories of bad Craigslist auditions. Have the directors done anything before? Do they have a website? Just save yourself the hassle. Save

Craigslist for finding roommates or selling your old headshots when you get famous.

The Importance of Non-Union Work

Eventually you will join the union (which will cost you over $3,000, as well as union dues of $198 every six months), but for now you are looking for *experience*, credits, "on the job" training, and great footage to use on your demo reel. Some of these non-union projects can be great, and some of them can be terrible and very disorganized (but honestly, that kind of happens with union projects as well). They are all looking for actors--music videos, web series, non-Equity showcases, plays, short films, student films, feature films, commercial specs, industrials, and even reality shows (yes, they cast those).

Make sure they give you copy when they are done editing! If you are working for free, they should at least give you your scenes to have for your demo reel. Sadly, I've heard too many stories of directors not giving the actors their footage, which I think is very unfair. If you have to, make the director sign a contract before you work saying he will give your footage two months after the film wraps. They should have no problem doing that. Take control of your career.

I've seen some amazing non-union student films, shot with better cameras than union films (simply because the students directing them have access to the school's incredibly expensive equipment, like the Red One camera). I've seen some terrible web series' that make no sense, have no storyline, are blurry, with terrible, poorly formatted scripts. You just never know. Do it, learn from it, and move on. Network, meet other actors, surround yourself with people who are as motivated as you are.

Joining the Union

The recently merged TV, film, commercial and voiceover union is called SAG-AFTRA. The theatre union is EQUITY. Ultimately, your goal is to be a part of these. The unions are there to protect actors, to make sure they are treated fairly, and to make sure they are compensated for their hard work in accordance to certain rules (overtime, child labor laws, meal penalty, etc.). All the big TV shows, Broadway plays, big commercials, and studio films are union projects that have guaranteed rates and working conditions for actors. Only join when you are ready! Many actors join SAG-AFTRA because they get "waivers" from doing extra work, pay the money, and suddenly they can't audition for all of the non-union work that is essential for building that resumé, demo reel, and most importantly, *confidence*. I've seen this happen too many times, and over eager actors end up stuck with no auditions and no work, simply because it sounded cool to join the union before they were ready. Most agents and casting directors don't care if you are in the union or not when they hire you for a TV show. They just want the right person for the job. If they hire you, you become a "must join," and then when you get your *second* union job (after 31 days), you have to pay the union fee before you show up to set. Then after you pay that hefty initiation fee, you then have to pay union dues every six months to stay in good standing with the union. Be smart! Once you book your first union job, then you become "union-eligible," which is a great place to be, as it allows you to seek out union and non-union work through the casting sites.

The Best Production Sites

Actors need to know what is filming in their area, who is casting, and what roles are available. You have to educate yourself, connect the dots, find out how these actors and directors are connected to each other, how they started out, and who represents them. Sites like Deadline Hollywood and Variety are wonderful for ways to find out what's currently filming. IMDb-Pro lets you look up any actor or project and find out their credits, their representation, and even how much money their movies made. Also check out the *Call Sheet* from *Backstage*, CastingAbout, the Black List, and Actor Genie. Watch every TV show that is being filmed in your city. Know the tone of the show and the types they are casting. Don't be lazy. If you want to break in, you have to know what you are "breaking into."

STEP 7: The Art of Auditioning

You just got called in for Creepy Guy #3 in a new student film that a director at NYU is doing for his thesis project. Great! Pop the champagne, start celebrating, pick out which car you are going to buy, and tell everyone you know. Not so fast.

Mastering the Room (phrase): The art of walking into a room with confidence, connecting to the reader, and convincing the casting director that you are perfect for the job.

The next step to breaking into acting is learning *how* to audition. The art of mastering "the room." Some people are great actors, and terrible auditioners. Some are great auditioners, but terrible actors. It is a skill, and one that must be learned and honed, just like any other kind of discipline. Audition technique, audition etiquette, and conquering nerves is an essential part of the process of breaking into acting, as this is where you get to show how good you are in front of the "decision-makers." Once you are on set, you have the luxury of being on location and having props and good actors working opposite you. In an audition, you have a chair. That's it. It much harder, and involves an active imagination.

Of course, you have to learn how to *act* before you audition. You don't want to put the cart before the horse, right? Don't go spending thousands of dollars at casting director workshops before you have a clue about what you are doing. That's how these businesses make money, and that's how you make a fool of yourself (more on that later). That's why on-camera training, business sense, and a fundamental understanding of the craft of acting are essential. You have to be honest with yourself about where you are in your career. Someday, you'll be one of those "offer only" actors, but for now you need to learn this essential skill in your pursuit to break in.

What to Expect in an On-Camera Audition

Auditions can be odd. They usually take place in a tiny room/office/living room with bad lighting and people staring at you while you do outrageous things to show them you are right for the part. I once had a commercial audition where I had to pretend to be dancing with an imaginary Pop Tart at a club while yelling "*Word up, Poppy!*" and doing the Cabbage Patch dance. Not kidding. Another time I had to be hooting and hollering while pretending to ride a mechanical bull, which was just a fold-up chair. Yet another time, I noticed casting director drawing a moustache on my headshot as I left a commercial audition. Good times! You have to commit to the circumstances, and somehow find the humor in doing it. You can sometimes feel like cattle, and that it is all a silly waste of time. But you never know when it's your turn, so you just have to keep yourself ready and focused, professional, and healthy mentally and physically. It's a numbers game. At some point it's going to hopefully go your way.

The Magic Light Bulbs

This one comes courtesy of actor Chris Diamantopoulos, who has starred in many TV shows and films:

> *One of the memorable auditions in which I put all my efforts into everything but actually preparing the material, was an appointment to read for a new TV series about mutants with super powers. The character could generate electricity with his hands. The audition material was several pages long and the role I was reading for did most of the talking. I had one day's notice to prepare, and instead of fully reading the sides, I spent the day at a magic store. I was looking to find a specialty light bulb that concealed a battery and could be turned on in ones hand. This, I thought, was "my way in!" I would show up at the casting and as the audition started, I would light my hands up and be fully in character.*
>
> *I cringe as I recall walking into the audition*

with something literally "up my sleeve." I made my way in front of the camera and on "action," my brilliant idea wouldn't "turn on." I tried in vain to covertly fiddle with the switch but to no avail. I was red and sweating, not only because I was in a room full of people staring at me, but also because it was August and I was wearing a heavy leather jacket to conceal my stupid trick that wouldn't work. The casting director reminded me that I had the first line and I stood there, knees shaking, with my face buried in the page trying to make sense of a scene I had scantly read. The audition trudged on, and as the scene neared its end, I was determined to get the light bulb to turn on and so I held the pages lower to obscure the vision of the casting director and with one final fidget, the bulb turned on as if to illuminate the dreadful performance. "What do you have in your jacket?" She asked, "is that... a...is that a light bulb? Why?" At this point I figured my handiwork had impressed them so I smugly nodded my head as if to say "You know it."

They just looked baffled, offered a perfunctory, dismissive thank you, and off I went thinking "I nailed that!"

The Casting Process

The Pre-Read--Typically your first audition will be with the *casting director* of the project. The pre-read. If it's for TV or film, they will usually have a camera set up to videotape the audition (to see what you look like on screen, and also in case they want to view it later or show it to the producer or director). Some shows cast the small roles directly from tape, without doing a callback. You can sit or stand, whatever makes you feel comfortable. Believe it or not, casting directors are on your side, and want you to do a good job. Usually they have you do a "Slate" to the camera before you start (You look into camera and say your name). Then you look at the reader *off*-camera (who is sitting right next to the camera) and begin the scene. If they sent you the sides beforehand, make sure you are fully prepared and can look up from the script and connect to the reader (very important!). If they ask you to do two monologues, make sure they are memorized and ready to go. When the audition is done, they may give you an adjustment and have you do it again, or they may just say "thank you." Then you go into the elevator, relive the audition over and over again, question the meaning of life, what their "thank you" meant, and don't sleep for three days.

The Callback--If the casting director likes you, they bring you back for the director, the writer, and/or the producers. You have passed the first hurdle of the casting director, and now you are being sent through to the decision makers. Wear *exactly* what you wore to the first audition, and don't change a thing with your read. You were called back based on what you did in the pre-read. If you are auditioning for a guest star or co-star, you usually will find out if you booked the job after a producer session (although sometimes they will do a *second* callback for a bigger guest starring role).

The Screen Test—If they are looking for a new series regular role on a pilot or a currently running show, you will usually have to go on to a screen test, both for the studio that is producing the show, and the network that is airing the show. The screen test usually takes place in a conference room, a small theatre, or sometimes you don't even have to be there, and they just show your audition tape in front of the executives (much better!). At this point in the audition, you have signed a huge contract stating how much money you will make, the size of your trailer, negotiated pay raises, and everything else. And you don't even have the job yet! It's between you and a few other people, and if you don't get the job, they just rip up your contract (good times!).

How to Nail an Audition

This is *your* time. The casting directors *want* you to be good. They are your friends, and they are on your side (so many actors forget that). You have about two minutes to convince them you are right for the job (but honestly they know in the first fifteen seconds if you are right or not). All that training now has to show itself in this one line, scene, or monologue. Know your lines, know whom you are talking to in the scene, know what you want from the other character, and figure out how to get it. They want to see a final, perfect, memorized performance, and they want to see your true personality, your *essence*, shine through. What are you fighting for? What is getting in the way? This is where training is crucial, as it gives you a safety net so you don't feel like you are floundering around up there. The rest is just being present enough to listen and respond to what is happening moment to moment in the scene, and bringing humanity and emotional truth to the circumstances. Any great acting school or coach can teach you that. If they give you an adjustment, be flexible and open to direction. They need to see that you can handle direction, and that you aren't so set in your ways.

Auditioning is an unusual way to gauge talent, but until someone finds a better solution, we all must go through it, and we all must learn to master it. We have to walk into a room of strangers and open ourselves up emotionally. We have to let down our guard and experience emotions, both through our eyes as well as our bodies. Actors who are considered "good in the room" can summon any emotion, however subtle, and be completely vulnerable and available in an audition situation, with no blocks, and no nerves. That is your goal, and that's what gets you work. Auditioning should be fun, not something that causes you anxiety. Nobody is forcing you to be there, so have fun! Until you are paying rent with your acting work, there should be no pressure whatsoever on you in the audition room. Think of auditions as a chance to play.

The 7 C's of Auditioning

Here are seven things that are essential to every good audition. If you keep these in mind, you will be grounded in the scene, focused, your nerves will dissolve, and you will stand out from the pack.

Confidence. If you don't believe in yourself, nobody else will. The audition starts the moment you walk into the room, so find a way to be relaxed, and project unshakeable confidence. If you don't have it, fake it. This is all about body language and eye contact, so walk into the room with your head up, shoulders back, with total focus and relaxation. It's the kind of confidence that makes people trust you, and allows them to feel they can put you on set or on stage tomorrow and you will be fine and not waste their time. You are prepared, know your job in the scene, your lines, and believe in the circumstances. Even if you are freaking out inside, you have to "act" like a confident person. (You are an actor, right?)

Character. Don't worry about what *they* are looking for. It's your job to show them your unique interpretation of who this character is. Your character has a point of view in the scene. What is it? Think of three adjectives to describe this person and write these at the top of the script (annoyed, frustrated, in love, etc.). If there is a chair in the room, how do they sit in this chair? What is the character's body language? How do they speak? The clearer you are on the character, the more your nerves dissolve, and you can disappear into this person's world.

Conflict. At the heart of every good scene is conflict, even if it's from within. What is at stake in the scene? What are the characters fighting for? What are the circumstances around this scene? Find out what that is, and put that nervous energy into how your character deals with it. If you are very clear on your conflict and objective, it will dictate the rhythm, inflection, and tone of each line, and avoid the trap of playing the "result."

Concentration. Take a breath before you begin the scene. Quiet your mind and concentrate on the moment before. This involves total emotional and physical commitment, to the character, to the words, the thoughts, and being totally prepared. It's not enough to just know the lines, you have to *live* them, and understand what's *behind* the lines. If you are worried about what people are thinking, or your next line, then you are not fully in the scene. Find a way to disappear into this world and make the reader the most important person in the room, so there isn't even room for you to be thinking about anything else. You have to be true to the emotions, and personalize them, so that your eyes, voice, and body are reflecting those feelings.

Connection. Eye contact. Look at the reader. Who is that person? How do you feel about them? What is that relationship like? It's important to listen in a very active way, as if you are hearing the words for the first time. It should feel like a real, improvised conversation, not a scene for an acting class. You have to absorb the lines and respond from moment to moment. It starts with the thought that triggers your first line, how you feel at the top of the scene, and where your character is coming from emotionally before he or she even starts speaking. It allows you to jump right into the scene with a strong connection. It should feel like you are the only two people in the room, and that we are witnessing a private conversation.

Clarity. Be clear with your choices. There is always more than one way to say a line. Pick one. This doesn't mean make bold, crazy, irrational choices, it just means make a decision with each line based on what your character wants. Don't be safe, and don't just glide over the important moments. Do the work at home, but then be open to direction and flexible on the room, in case you are given an adjustment. What is your character saying? What is he *not* saying?

Charisma. This is what makes good auditions stand out. It's your essence, your personality, your authentic self. It's what you have that nobody else can offer, even when everyone is reading the same exact script. It's the magic that you bring to the lines that make them interesting, unique, and different, with your own spin on it. It's that fire in your eyes, alive and energetic, the thought "behind the eyes"—the art of getting people to want to watch you. I think all actors should read *The Charisma Myth* by Olivia Fox Cabane to truly understand what it means to have this.

The Cold-Read

We've all been there. You get a big television or film audition, and you have a day (Yay!) or even several (Wow!) to work on it. You tell everyone on Facebook about it, you memorize it, work on your backstory, you go through all of Uta's questions, maybe even do a movement journal (just me?), come up with wonderful "bold" choices, write out your subtext, your action adverbs, meet with a coach (or several), and then you show up and they give you a completely different script! Um…what?!

"The sides for this character have changed"
or *"You are more right for this other character. Go*

47

out and work on the new sides for ten minutes and come back in," or *"You know what? Why don't you just give this a read right now."*

Ten minutes? What's an actor to do? Cue panic, sweaty palms, and scrambling to make sense of the script. All that work you did just went out the window, and now you have to make quick choices and impress them with very little preparation. Before you jump out the window of that tiny little casting office, fire your coach, yell at your agent, and completely freak out, take a deep breath and realize that they are on your side, and this is where your cold-read training kicks in.

Here are 10 tips to nail the cold-read. Print this out, laminate it, put it in your headshot folder, share it, save it on your desktop, staple it to your forehead. You will be doing cold-reads for the rest of your career, so you must master it.

Answer the big questions. Who am I? What do I want? Who am I talking to and how do I *feel* about him or her? Where am I? (A crowded bar, an interrogation room, a park.) This is what drives the scene and creates the circumstances for the scene to come to life. Write it at the top so you don't forget.

Circle the little moments. A look, a smile, an uncomfortable silence, a kiss, etc. Sometimes the moments *between* the lines are just as important. Don't be afraid of pauses. You can say so much about a character's history with one look, one eye roll, one justified pause.

Figure out what just happened. In television and film, scenes usually start in the middle. What happened right before your first line? What did someone *just* say to you? Your first line is always a *response.* Figure out where your character is coming from and what emotional level to start at. Do you start the scene angry? How angry on a scale of one to ten? I write down a number to calibrate my character's emotions at the top of the scene.

Memorize your first and last line. So important. Establish that connection right away with your eyes. This starts the scene on a great note, with eye contact and confidence, even if you have no idea what your next line is.

Dog-ear the pages. Nothing kills a cold-read more than that awkward silence when an actor is struggling to turn the page. A simple fold at the bottom right of the page will make it easier to stay in the scene, flip the page, and keep the momentum moving. Or even write down your next line at the bottom of the page.

Employ the 80/20 rule. Eighty percent of your attention on the reader, twenty percent on the script. Follow along with your thumb, and every time you look down, grab your line quickly and come right back up. Think of your script as a rubber band that bounces your eyes back up immediately. You will never lose your place this way. The more you look down, the more we see your eyelids, the more you lose your audience and interrupt the important moments.

Listen, listen, listen! This is so important. Once you say your line, be interested in the response. Take a two second pause before you look down. A lot of actors forget this in their effort to get to the next line. It's just as much about the other person's lines as it is about yours. Even if there is a pause before you get your next line, as least you are *listening* in the scene and absorbing what is being said (as we do in real life).

Don't "death grip" the script. Be confident and relaxed—hold the script in front of you with one hand (so you can look down quickly with your *eyes* when necessary, and not your *whole head* like a "bobble-head actor"). Avoid the famous two-handed, desperate, white knuckle "I'm gonna win an Oscar!" death grip. *Act* like you've had the script for weeks. Look the reader in the eyes (not for too long; it's creepy), take a breath, and find that chemistry to make the scene come to life.

Stay in character. Allow for mistakes. You will most likely get hung up on words. Simply stay in character when you are turning the page, looking for your next line, without any kind of apology or awkward facial expression. That is being a true professional. Be present for two minutes.

Find the emotion. The emotion is more important than the lines. Sure, it's important to say the writer's words, but if everyone is reading the same lines, you have to find your unique spin on those lines, your opinion about the lines, and what emotion is brewing underneath (and how your character is *masking* it). That is where the lines come from, and in a cold-read, you have to come up with that choice quickly.

At the end of the day, auditioning is acting. We can worry all day about props, miming, clothing, eye-lines, frame, and everything else under the sun, but truly casting directors are looking for you to *be* the character. If you are wearing a blue shirt instead of a grey shirt, I promise you won't lose a job over it.

The Self-Taped Audition

More and more auditions are self-taped. It gives actors a lot of freedom over their auditions, it's a controlled environment, and as a result, the auditions are more relaxed. Now, you really have to master this skill, as many actors book jobs directly from tape. A lot of actors don't pay enough attention to this. I'm talking out of focus, poorly lit, unprofessional, shaky, Blair Witch-style auditions with your mom or roommate doing their best Tara Reid impression off-camera.

I get it. You get the tape request at the last minute, panic, and need to make some quick decisions. What do you do when it's 10:30 p.m. on a Monday, you're out celebrating your roommate's 49th birthday party, and your agent emails you saying they need the tape by the next morning? You can either pay a lot of money to get it done professionally, frantically call your film school friends looking for a camera and desperately try to rent a rehearsal space last minute, or you can simply take a deep breath, and do it at home using the tools you already have. I promise you, it's not that complicated. Here are a few simple ways to make a professional, quality, competitive self-taped audition.

Use your iPhone or iPad. We all have one of these, and the HD quality is better than most camcorders. Prop it up on a book, or buy a cheap tripod ($20 on Amazon), and an iPhone tripod clip ($8). You can email the file directly from the phone afterwards, instead of uploading to WeTransfer or Dropbox. It couldn't be easier.

Use a neutral backdrop. A blank wall works best. Or buy an inexpensive gray or blue bed sheet and pin it on the wall. Keep it simple and clutter free. Nobody needs to see your creepy doll collection in the background.

Find a quiet room. Turn the TV off, silence your phone, tell your roommate to stop singing, and shut the windows. Nothing kills a self-tape more than car alarms, barking dogs, and sirens.

No shadows. Don't use overhead lighting, as it creates strong shadows under your eyes and chin. Use natural light, or if your apartment is dark, buy a couple of cheap clip-on lights from your hardware store. Put the lights a little above eye level, on either side of the camera, and use daytime fluorescent bulbs (tungsten bulbs create a less appealing "candlelight" effect). It's all about the eyes, so make sure they are clearly lit and in focus.

Get a good reader. A bad reader or a loud reader can really ruin an audition tape. Unless your roommate or dad is Christian Bale, find someone who is an actor (a good one) to sit off-camera and read the scene with you. Make sure when they are reading they are quieter than you, as they will be right next to the camera, and you want the voices to balance out. Also, make sure the reader doesn't read the stage directions. You'd think that would be obvious. You'd be surprised.

Check the slate instructions. Sometimes the casting director wants something very specific with the slate, like a full body shot, or a tight close-up and profiles. Make sure you read the original email carefully. If the instructions are to send via YouTube or Vimeo, make sure it's a *private* link. If you are uploading into iMovie, you can send directly to Vimeo or YouTube from that application.

Slate separately. It's always better to separate the slate and the scenes, and film as separate takes. It allows a break so you can really get into the character before rolling the camera for your first scene. The slate is done directly into camera (name, age, role, agency, etc.). The scenes are to the reader sitting *next* to the camera. Also, don't slate in character. It's weird. This is the first time anyone sees you. Be cool, be natural—be someone they would want to work with.

Use a tight medium frame. The frame should be from the chest up. Be still. Think it and feel it, and the camera will capture it. Save the flailing chicken acting for your *Guys and Dolls* audition. Don't pan, and don't do any handheld *Law and Order* stuff. Lock the frame and keep it simple. Too much movement is distracting from the performance. The camera should be at eye level, not below, not above, and there should be a little room above your head.

Sit or stand. It's a medium shot, so it doesn't matter, unless it affects your energy. Sometimes if you stand it gives you the scene more life, as a chair or sofa tends to zap the energy. Go with whatever feels right.

Eye lines. Never look directly into the camera in a scene unless the stage directions specifically say so. Make the reader the main character in the scene, and connect to that person. If there is another character, imagine someone standing directly on the other side of camera.

Set a time limit. Half-hour to an hour max. Don't overthink it. Be as prepared as possible when you start taping (memorized, strong choices), so that you don't waste time messing up lines. Do two or three takes of each scene, and pick only the best one to send (unless otherwise requested). We're not doing a David Fincher movie.

Always watch it back before sending. You never know if there will be a tech problem. Make sure it looks and sounds good, and is in focus. You want this to be as professional as possible.

Look your best. Treat it like a real audition. Make yourself camera ready (hair, makeup, outfit), and make sure you are well rested. Treat it like you are walking into a screen test. Trust me, it matters.

Finally, just relax and have fun. The great thing about self-taping is you can do it until you get it right. If you send a bad self-tape audition, it reflects poorly on you and makes you look amateur. You want to be as professional as possible, and show the people hiring you that you take your job seriously. If you follow these steps, your talent, not your poor tape quality, will stand out. Since most of us have this technology at our fingertips, learn how to make the best use of it and be prepared when that big opportunity comes along.

Dealing with Nerves

We have all been there—in the sitting area, waiting to go in for the big audition, mind racing, hands sweating, obsessively reading over our sides, hoping and praying that we don't totally mess up, pass out, get bad feedback, get dropped by our agents, and give up on the business. No? Just me?

Here's the thing. Everyone gets nervous. Even experienced actors get nervous. Let's face it: auditioning is inherently awkward, but it's all about how you *handle* nerves that allows you to deliver a good audition. Here are some techniques I use for myself and with my students, to get relaxed before an audition.

Make an audition playlist. Put twenty songs on your phone that make you feel calm and relaxed. Listen to them from the moment you step out your door until the moment they call your name. Stay focused—avoid email, Instagram and Facebook. Allow the music to simply quiet the mind.

Take 10 deep breaths. Just close your eyes, and for four seconds each: inhale, hold, and exhale. With every inhale, repeat "relax" to yourself in your mind (or out loud, if you want to be weird). When you exhale, imagine all the stress leaving your body. If people think you are crazy, good. Let them be intimidated.

Be prepared. Memorize the lines so well, in so many different ways, that they become second nature to you. It's muscle memory, just like practicing a routine in dance. Practice with a friend many times. You don't want the audition to be the first time you hear the words out loud.

Visualize the audition. This one works wonders for people. After rehearsing the scene many times, close your eyes and visualize the audition from start to finish. Imagine walking in the door, fully prepared, slating your name, and then disappearing into the scene, completely forgetting about the fact that it's an audition. Then imagine walking away and feeling great about it. This can be a powerful tool if used effectively.

Walk in with confidence. You are an actor, right? Act like a confident person. It's all about body language. Hold your head high, make eye contact, bring your shoulders back, and *act* like you already have the job. Even if you are nervous, you will make the casting director feel comfortable, and your nerves will dissolve.

It's really just a chance to play, right? Stay present and have fun!

Simply listen. A lot of actors forget this. In the audition room it's your job to fully immerse yourself in the scene and really listen as if you are hearing the words for the first time. In your mind, you should be thinking *"What did that character just say to me? How do I feel about that?"* instead of *"God, I hope I don't mess up. Did I put enough pomade in my hair?"*

You can only act, take direction, and do well in an audition if you are able to manage your nerves so you can feel comfortable and relaxed.

The Fastest Ways to Memorize Lines

What's the best way to memorize quickly? Perhaps you have twelve pages of sides for a callback tomorrow morning, or you have to memorize a two-hour play in a week because someone just dropped out, or maybe you signed up for a casting director pay-to-meet, and at the last minute decided to memorize a really overdone monologue from *Mean Girls* (Just me?).

You have no idea how you are going to learn the lines this quickly. Maybe you've tried putting the script under your pillow hoping to learn the lines by osmosis (doesn't work), or you've tried having your four roommates sing your lines to you at three in the morning (totally creepy). You've tried everything, and it doesn't work. What do you do? The old method of covering your lines with your hand never seems to work, as the lines always feel like they are on the surface, and not ingrained—sort of like cramming for a math test—and will be out the window the second you finish.

I've tried many different ways over the years, and I found these are by far the quickest ways to memorize lines.

The *Rehearsal* app. This is hands down my favorite way for actors to learn lines. It's the scene partner that never gets tired of running lines with you. If you can get past the fact that it's $19.99, this is a game changer. You can highlight the lines in the app, record the other character's lines, and use it as a teleprompter, which will scroll through the script as you are reading it. Then it just keeps playing on a loop. The secret for me is to *whisper* my lines and read the other character's lines *out loud* when I'm recording, so I don't get too caught up in the *way* I'm saying my lines, but I know how much time I have to say them. I will literally put my iPad on a chair and pretend I'm running lines with someone. It's so much better than a tape recorder. Love it. (Time: Approx. 30 minutes for a 12-page scene.)

Write them out. This is quicker than you think, and you always remember the lines word for word when you are done. I have used this for memorizing longer scenes with lots of speeches. I find this works really well because you are connecting your mind to the action of writing the lines down and seeing the lines at the same time. They seem to go to a deeper part of your brain. I prefer writing them by hand instead of typing.

Write out *just your lines* in one big paragraph, then run through the scene out loud. Then do this five more times, breaking your lines into thoughts each time. The last time you write them out, see if you can do it without looking at the script, and just think of the other person's lines. What's great about it is that you aren't memorizing what the *other* characters are saying, and can really listen in the scene and not anticipate the lines. (Time: Approx. one hour for a 12-page scene.)

Run the lines with someone many times. Preferably an actor, not your friend who was an extra on *Blue Bloods* one time, likes to coach you, and keeps reading the stage directions out loud. The first time you run through it, just *listen* to the words. Focus on pausing between each line, really absorbing what's being said and going over the scene many times in many different ways, playing with intention, actions, and pacing. Try it sitting and standing, and allow yourself to make mistakes and explore every way *not* to do it, while also getting more and more comfortable with the lines. Focus on the "why" and the circumstances, which will help you learn the scene on a deeper level. If you forget your lines, you can find your way back because you really understand what's going on. (Time: 30 minutes to an hour.)

Personally, I usually use a combination of these three techniques to prepare for every audition. I will write down the lines, then run them with the *Rehearsal* app, then with another actor, during which time I will speed through them as fast as I can (the real test to see how well you know them). After that I will improvise the lines, and see if I can come up with some added moments and reactions *between* the lines that feel authentic to me, in a way that I would say them. Then I layer the writer's words back on and blend it all together. This way, I am memorized, but also flexible and open to direction and change.

At the end of the day you want the lines to seem like second nature, genuine and authentic, as if they are coming from a real person with real thoughts and ideas. Auditions cause anxiety, and while you may have them memorized at home, when you walk into the room it's easy to get distracted and forget. As actors, we need to prepare for this, and be very, very memorized (but not locked into a pattern), so that we are confident, relaxed, committed, listening, and open to direction.

Handling Rejection

A lot of the time we won't be right for the part. We will deal with tons of rejection. That comes with the territory. There are thousands more actors than there are roles. So you must get used to getting rejected, and not take it personally. Sometimes it's about you having the wrong hair color, being too old, too young or too big, etc. You can't control it, so let it go, dust yourself off, stay focused, and move on to the next. If you keep putting out good work, you will book jobs eventually. Casting directors remember actors who audition well. It's a numbers game.

Auditioning is your job, getting the role is the icing on the cake. You may go on tons of auditions before you get your first job. If you are wrong for the part, but are a total pro in the audition, and deliver an amazing read, they will remember you and bring you in for the *next* project they are doing. It's about winning over the room, the casting director, doing good work *consistently*, and treating everyone nicely along the way. You never know if that casting director or casting associate or assistant will be the producer (aka "decision maker") on your next project. So leave your excuses at the door (sick, hung over, trains were running behind, my dog ate my script, didn't have enough time to look at it, acting isn't fun anymore), and walk in that room and show them you can handle *anything*. If you think an audition is stressful, it is way more stressful on an actual set (more on that later).

STEP 8: Demo Reels and Footage

Once you book a bunch of jobs, and have some amazing footage, you need to make a demo reel. It is *essential*. Everyone asks for it. Audition websites allow you to upload them (which will get you more auditions because you show up higher in search results), agents ask for them, casting directors request them when you are up for a job. It the easiest way for a casting director or an agent to see what you are about before calling you in for a meeting or an audition.

> **Demo reel (noun): a short, engaging, 1-2 minute "sizzle" reel containing your best on screen TV and film work.**

It is a movie trailer for *you*, and it should be professional and concise, and show off what you do best. Google "actor's demo reels" and you'll find some examples of professional acting reels (some good, and some bad).

The Contents of a Good Demo Reel

A typical reel is about one to two minutes, and should have about 4 scenes on it. It should start with your headshot, then fade into your name and *contact* info (you'd be amazed at how many actors forget this), then start with your scene with the highest production value first. "Production value" means the scene *looks* good and *sounds* good. It could be a student film, it could be a meaty scene on *Glee*. Each scene should focus on *you*, and be no more than thirty seconds. When I say it should focus on *you*, I mean it can't be a scene with one minute of someone else talking, and you only have one line. It shouldn't include *featured* work, and it *definitely* can't be you as an extra on *The Good Wife*. Decision makers need to see what you look like on-camera, how you act, and how you command the screen.

A good demo reel shows your type and how you'd realistically be cast for TV and film. Go through all of your footage (which should be uploaded and saved on your computer, as you will always be updating your reel), and see which scenes best suit your type, and condense it into an amazing little movie that showcases your talent. You can use student films, web series, or even professionally filmed auditions and scenes. Just make sure it showcases *you*. There are companies out there that you can *pay* to produce and film an entire scene for you, specifically so you can put it on the demo reel. They will write it, hire the actors, direct it, edit it, and give it back to you. However, I'm a big fan of actors saving money, and not trying to skip steps and go the easy route. Try to get work yourself first, go on tons of auditions, learn the ropes, work on some student films and test the waters.

Remember, you are the CEO of your own business. The demo reel is your ticket to the next level. As you get more and better credits, you will trim out the lower quality stuff. Just like on your resumé. If you have a bunch of low budget student films when you are starting out, that's fine! A lot of student films are shot on amazing cameras, and look fantastic. Just don't put *everything* you have on there. Pick and choose what represents you the best way—the best acting, and good coverage (close-ups, two shots, etc.). Ask a coach for guidance, as it always helps to get an outside observer. Maybe it's time to cut that Shakespeare monologue that you did right into camera in an extreme close-up (Blair Witch style).

Gathering Footage

A lot of actors work for free on non-union jobs and never get their footage. Why? Well, the directors are lazy, they move on to other projects, they never finish the film, and a myriad of other reasons that I have heard over the years. It's extremely unprofessional, and really disrespectful for actors who have taken time off from their jobs to work on a student film for free. That being said, I highly recommend actors in the non-union world make the director sign a one page contract saying they are responsible for getting them the footage by a certain deadline (a reasonable date set after the film is edited). This is only fair, as too many times I've seen actors do amazing work and then never get a copy of their footage that was promised to them. Have some dignity, speak up for yourself. This is about networking, and beginning relationships, and the director who doesn't give the footage will be remembered down the road when you are well known and he wants to try and get you in for his project. "You never gave me my footage, bro."

Obviously, with network and cable TV, it's much easier than ever to get footage, as we all have access to DVR's, iTunes, Netflix, and other sites to instantly access footage from an episode or film we appeared in. iSpot.tv is a great site to get a copy of your commercial once it has aired. *Handbrake* is a wonderful software tool that allows an actor to "capture" footage from a DVD, and use it to upload to their demo reel.

Learn to Edit Your Own Reel

If you have a Mac, I highly recommend using iMovie to edit your own reel, as it will save you hundreds if not thousands of dollars down the road. Take charge of your career. I went to one of those free iMovie seminars at the Apple store, learned how to do it, and have never looked back. I can spend all day editing my own footage, uploading a new version of my demo reel to YouTube, and never pay anyone another cent.

Creating Your Own Content

A lot of actors feel frustrated by how long it takes to get their footage, or how few auditions they are getting. This is where self-producing comes in. Again, it's all about not being lazy, building the career that you want for yourself, and not sitting back and being at the mercy of whether or not there are roles for you. Write the roles yourself. Write a short scene, and film it. You can rent camera equipment, but honestly, so many consumer cameras now can be used for this purpose. If you have an interesting idea, and have talented friends (writers, actors, directors), get everyone together and talk about creating a *webseries*. I guarantee you people will jump at the opportunity. These days creating your own content is essential, as actors have access to affordable equipment, editing software, and everything else they would need to create a wonderful short episode or film and immediately post to the internet.

Upload the final demo reel to YouTube or Vimeo. If you have iMovie, it's as simple as clicking a button. Find the scenes you like, from your footage or self-produced content, cut them down, and upload into a one to two minute clip. You want an easy, simple, email-able link that you can send to anyone on a moment's notice, post a link to on your business card, your website, your IMDb page, and your email signature. The last thing you want is to get a meeting with an agent, only to have him say "*Send me your demo reel,*" and you say "*Uh, I don't have one made yet.*" It's very unprofessional, and you pretty much just shot yourself in the foot.

STEP 9: Your Online Presence

It's easier than ever for actors to get their names out there, thanks to YouTube and social media sites like Instagram, Facebook and Twitter. This is where you get to post your headshot, resumé, demo reel, and website for all of your fans to see, and also engage with industry people in an organic way. Some casting directors post auditions on these sites, and some agents bring in actors from these sites for possible representation (true story). Some actors gain lots of followers and get discovered from their self-produced videos or webseries' going viral. Social media is an amazing marketing tool, and it's essential for breaking into acting. You never know who is going to see your picture and resumé on one of these sites and call you in for an audition. I've seen it happen!

You have to think of yourself as an entrepreneur and work on building your personal brand.

Buy Your Domain

Check out a site like *GoDaddy*, which allows you to check if your website domain name is available. Ideally yourfullname.com. For around $13/year, you can hold the rights to your own domain name, and even add a personal email address to it for a few dollars more. It's very simple. If your full name isn't available, try adding "actor" to the end of it (i.e. mattnewtonactor.com) or put a dash in the middle (matt-newton.com). You want it to be easy for people to find you.

Make a Website

Every actor should have a website. It is the easiest way to have all of your info in one place. It will go on your business cards, your resumé, your social media pages, your IMDb page, and everything else. It should be simple, concise, and to the point. It should include your headshots, resumé, demo reel, contact info, news, and anything else you think might be interesting about you. You never know who will be looking at your website. Treat it like a work of art. A good, professional website speaks volumes about you, and shows people that are you a total pro.

Gone are the days of paying someone thousands to do this. Check out *Squarespace* and *Weebly* for free website design (with great layouts), which allow you to create an elegant website for free, and they will also host it for you. They allow you to attach the website to the domain name that you purchased. You will constantly be making changes to your website (updating your demo reel, your resumé, your headshots), and you don't want to have to pay someone every time. Trust me. On this website, you should have a front landing page (no flash please) that has your headshot and an embedded demo reel. On a separate page you should have a PDF of your resumé (for easy downloading and viewing), a page for headshots, a bio page, a review page, and a contact page with social media links. Simple, easy, and professional. Link to your IMDb page, if you have one, as that is the main way that casting directors look up actors.

Make a YouTube Channel.

If you have some amazing performances, or have links to student films you've done, or a self-produced comedy series with your friends, make a YouTube channel under your name. Put all of your good stuff there. It can give you great web exposure, and you can build a fan base. It's a long shot, but some people get discovered this way. Especially if the work is amazing, and organically finds its way around the internet (i.e. without you *begging* people to email it to everyone they know).

Join Twitter.

Create a twitter account with your headshot, a link to your website and your IMDb page, and start networking. *Backstage*, Actors Access, and certain casting directors post links to auditions on Twitter. You can network, meet casting directors (in a non creepy way), ask questions, get advice, build fans, post your work, and build an wonderful online community for yourself, while also keeping people updated on what you are working on. It's a great way to get immediate answers from people in the know, if you do it the right way. It's a very powerful tool. The key is to not nag them, and not ever ask them to bring you in. Let your work speak for itself.

Create a Facebook Fan Page.

Set up a separate page separate from your personal Facebook page, that is just about you "the actor," not you "the party animal out on a bender." This is where you might post new headshots, short films you have been in, movie screenings, info about new projects, and anything else relevant to your career. It's about establishing relationships and nurturing them in an organic way, without saying "Please bring me in for an audition." Don't "friend" a casting director unless you know them. It makes them uncomfortable, and you don't want to be brought in for them and have to ask the awkward question, *"Why didn't you accept my Friend Request?"*

STEP 10: Agents and Managers

"If only I had an agent...."

You can't have a professional acting career without some kind of representation, whether it be an agent or a manager. But there is nothing easy about getting one. It's simple supply and demand. There are way more actors than agents and managers need. If casting directors are the gatekeepers, agents and managers are the ones that get you in front of that gate. These are the people whose job it is to get you paid work (so they get paid), and to get you into rooms with the big decision makers. There are about one hundred and twenty talent agencies in New York (and about the same in Los Angeles) that cover everything from actors and magicians, to comedians and babies. Some have fifty clients, some have five hundred. They have long-standing relationships with casting directors, producers, directors, studios, acting teachers, and everyone else in the business. They are on your team, they are your negotiators, your father, your mother, and your best friend. Some people talk to their managers more than their families.

Agent vs. Manager

Talent agents are licensed by the state, bonded, and take a ten percent cut of whatever you make. You never, ever pay an agency up front. If they ask you to pay up front, walk away. That ten percent cut is an agent's incentive to pick up the phone and get you auditions. If you make money, they make money. It's a win win. They have pre-established relationships with casting directors, and they can push for you if they really believe in you. They are the middle man, and without them, you would not have access to these high profile roles. Usually they make you sign a one year contract (with a ninety day "out clause" if they don't get you auditions within that time), and they can represent anywhere from 100-500 clients. Some are bi-coastal with dozens of agents in each office in New York and Los Angeles, and some are boutique agencies with a few agents, and there are some with one agent, operating in one office, with no assistant (and usually represents a lot of actors in the ensemble of a Broadway show).

Managers are smaller, unregulated (unless they choose to join the Talent Manager's Association), and charge between ten percent and twenty percent, which is paid in addition to the agent fee (if you have both). Managers can have as few as ten clients, and will most likely want you to sign for three years, and are there more to oversee your career long-term, look through your headshot proofs, pick you up off the ground when you are depressed, guide you with your marketing tools, help steer you in the right direction and find the right appointments for you, push really hard for you when you are right for a project, and in general will work in tangent with an agent as an extra push for their actors. They have different connections. That being said, there are agents that hate working with managers, and agents that love managers. Do you need both? It depends where you are in your career. In L.A. and New York, managers are very common, and potentially a great way for actors to get their foot in the door, as managers are more open to "developmental" clients like yourself, who don't have an established career yet. Until you are making your agents lots of money, you are considered "developmental," and your career is in the *infancy* stage.

A casting director posts breakdowns via *Breakdowns Express* and agents push for their clients to get in the room and be seen. An agent who really believes in you will fight to the end to prove that you are right for the job. When they get you an audition, you better deliver in the room. Agents negotiate your pay rates, the size of your trailer, your backend points, your housing for your national tour of *Cats,* your bonus if the show is a hit, everything. There are *theatrical* agents (TV, film, theatre), and there are *commercial* agents. There are also voiceover agents, modeling agents, pet agents, and other kinds of agents, but let's focus theatrical and commercial.

Big vs. Small

There are different levels of theatrical agents (or "legit" agents). Corporate refers to the big ones that represent the stars (UTA, William Morris Endeavor, CAA, ICM). Some of the next largest agencies (bicoastal) are Gersh, Paradigm, Resolution, APA, Innovative, Abrams, and Don Buchwald. These agents can have hundreds of clients who travel back and forth between both coasts, they have established talent, TV stars transitioning to film and vice versa, and probably reality stars who are trying to parlay their fame into big money speaking engagements, stunt casting on TV shows (where they offer a role to a actor/reality star to boost ratings), and whatever else they can milk out of their fifteen minute of fame. Then there are the smaller "boutique" agencies (Leading Artists, Stone Manners, Harden Curtis, and Talent Works are wonderful examples). These agencies have some TV stars, and a lot of their actors are probably on Broadway in some capacity. Some of these agencies have "Youth Divisions," which specialize in kids and teens and young adults (up to age 25 or 30), and some represent eighteen and over only. There are even smaller agencies (one agent and one assistant) who have loyal clients, and although they aren't huge, they could be wonderful for you. It all depends what you are looking for, and what you need.

Freelancing vs. Signing

In New York it's somewhat common for agents to "freelance" with actors before signing. In L.A. this is nonexistent. When you freelance, you aren't under contract, and have the ability to work with several agents at once. It means they are "trying you out," but are still far more focused on their signed clients. If you get callbacks or book a bunch of jobs for them, then they will probably offer you a contract. If they get you an audition, and you book it, of course you have to pay them ten percent. That's just etiquette. In a perfect world (which it rarely is) you really want someone to sign you and really give you the attention you deserve, who will really believe in you and your talent.

Commercial Agents

Commercial agents can represent up to two hundred and fifty or more actors. Sometimes a big theatrical agency will also have a commercial division (on-camera, voiceover, beauty, print, and hosting), and want to sign you across the board, and sometimes only the commercial division will be interested in you. Perhaps you are really attractive and marketable, have no experience, and want to start with a commercial agent and book some regional or national spots before crossing over to film, TV and theatre (That's what my sister did). The best way into a mid-level agency is through their commercial division. Target some commercial agents that may be right for you. Maybe you'll book a huge national network campaign, you'll become instantly recognizable, and that will be the way you break into acting. Everyone's path is different. There are no golden rules in this business. That being said, booking commercials isn't easy. Some people go out on hundreds of commercial auditions before they book one.

Commercial agents are looking for types. Yes, it's still about talent, and you have to be able to walk into a room and deliver lines better than anyone else, but it's also very much about *type*. It's not about you, it's about the product. Advertisers are hiring actor *types* to market *products* to customers all over the country. They are more interested in you being able to appeal to a wide audience, than whether or not you did Shakespeare in a parking lot. Commercial agents and casting directors LOVE improv training. So if you can get into class at the Pit, Groundlings, or Upright Citizens Brigade, then you should pursue that route. I always recommend that older actors who are just starting out take a good commercial audition class, as that will give them a real sense of what is required of them in that marketplace, from a casting director's perspective, and the types of commercials that may be right for.

How to Find an Agent

Which agent is right for you? Do your research. My favorite agent research tools are Henderson's *New York Agencies* (a once monthly book that you can get at the Drama Bookshop with updated addresses and lists of agents), and the *New York Agent Book* by K Callan, which contains a thorough description of every agent in New York, what they specialize in, and who they represent. Another great tool for research is IMDb-Pro, which allows you to look up any agent by their name, see who they represent, and what each of their clients have done, along with their headshot. It's an amazing tool, and will really give you a good sense if an agency is right for you or not, and the caliber of talent on their roster.

Referrals

The *best* way to get an agent or manager is a referral. If you know someone with an agent, and they want to put in a good word for you and drop off your headshot, great. If a casting director loves you and wants to set you up with an agent, even better. Use any and every connection you can. Or maybe you are in a play with another actor, who wants to refer you to their agent. Or maybe that agent comes to the play, sees how wonderful you are, and calls you in for a meeting. Word of mouth is very powerful.

Hard Copy Mailings

Agents' offices are flooded with headshots that actors have mailed in. It's sort of a blind way of sending any agent in town your marketing materials. All actors do this, and some get meetings from it, especially if they have a wonderful, concise cover letter and are young and hot. It's as simple as buying a sheet of mailing labels from the Drama Book Shop and blanketing the town with your stuff. I really, really don't recommend this, as I think actors need to save their money and be smarter about how they present themselves, and target the agents that are the right fit for them.

So let's say you have narrowed down your list to twenty agents and managers that you think are right for you (based on your research on IMDb-Pro, your demo reel, your age, your credits, and your marketability), and want to send out your headshots. The best time to do this is between June and July, and between Thanksgiving and Christmas. Why? Because that is when most TV shows are on hiatus from casting and agents have more time to look for new people. However, now that Amazon, Netflix and Hulu are creating original content all the time, agents and managers are busier year round, and there is less of an "off season."

Cover Letter

When you send out your headshot and resumé, you include a cover letter, which includes your most recent bookings, where you study, and what you are looking for in an agency.

A basic typed cover letter should look like this (regular font, regular size paper):

Dear Mr. Francis,

I recently graduated from Vassar College with a Drama degree, and am currently seeking theatrical representation. I am currently enrolled in an advanced on-camera acting class at MN Acting Studio, I booked my third student film this month, and was recently called in by Melissa Moss for a Blue Bloods audition. My headshot, resumé, demo reel, and website link are attached.

I think your agency would be good fit for me, and I would love to set up a meeting. I look forward to hearing from you.

Sincerely,

Matt Newton
www.mattnewton.com

That's it. No stuff about "I think I'm a really good actor," or "What's up? I just got out of jail," or "People tell me I look like Honey Boo Boo." Half the time they don't even read it anyway, but you do *need* to have one. And it needs to have conversation pieces on there—what you recently booked, where you went to school, what casting director you know, or what actor you know that they represent. Something that might catch their eye in a sea of hundreds of cover letters and headshots. Oh, and please make sure you use correct grammar and spell check it. Nothing says amateur like a short cover letter with fragmented sentences and misspelled words.

You may hear from them in two days, you may hear from them in three months, maybe you won't hear at all. But this is the first step in getting them to notice you, and you must do it in a professional manner. Especially if you have no referrals. Remember, there are tons of actors out there who want agents, so it's essential that your marketing tools are amazing. If the agent does open your envelope (more likely the assistant), they will first look at your headshot, then your resumé, and then they may even pull up your website. Have all of your bases covered!

DON'T call the agent (they hate that), stop by their office and ask for a meeting, or hand write your cover letter and attach it to a creepy 4x6 shot of you in your living room. Some people put glitter in the envelope or send the headshot in architectural tubes to "stand out" (not kidding). Yes, people do all of these things. It reeks of amateur, and stinks of desperation. Keep it professional.

Emailing/Stalking Agents

A lot of agents' email addresses are now available online, or are published in these agent books. Unless they specifically say they accept email submissions, I would avoid unsolicited emails to agents at all costs. The only reason you should email an agent is if you have a direct referral from one of their clients, and you put that client's name in the subject so it gets their attention. Otherwise it goes right to their junk mail. Agents get so many emails during the day from their own clients and casting directors, that they will most likely skip right over or not even see your email if you send it. It's not professional. Don't do it. Even if you "accidentally" found it on Google. And I would also avoid leaving long voicemails on their machine late at night listing all of your credits (it happens).

Pay-to-Meet Workshops

You've seen the ads: All you have to do is pay some money, read some commercial copy, a monologue, or a scene of your choice, and suddenly you too could be signed by an agent or be offered an audition for a hit TV show. "*Just pay $50 and you can have five minutes with the agent or casting director of your* *choice! Your big break is right around the corner!"* Sounds too good to be true, right?

There is a lot of controversy around these "Pay-to-Meet" workshops, and whether or not actors should fork over their hard earned cash to meet casting directors and agents. The company websites brag about all of the actors who have been called in or signed from them. Some actors think it provides them an opportunity for that rare "in-person submission"—the chance for them to meet that big agent or casting director, do a scene for them, charm them, and show them how talented they are. Other actors feel that it is a waste of money—that we should earn the right to be in front of an agent or casting director, and that paying for an opportunity seems like a scam.

The truth is, pay-to-meet workshops have become a necessary evil. Some agents even suggest their own clients sign up for certain casting workshops, as it gives that actor a chance to develop a relationship, so it's easier for that agent to get them in the room when a specific audition comes up. There are some casting directors who *only* call in actors who they meet in workshops (truth). But what about all of those actors who don't have agents, who spend thousands of dollars on these workshops (yes, thousands) and end up with nothing except an empty wallet and a whole lot of tears?

I've often heard stories from ill-prepared actors who sign up for a ton of these hoping for that big break, only to end up incredibly disappointed (not to mention poor). It seems that some actors think they can skip all of the steps, and the hard work, training, and resumé building that goes into pursuing this career. While the services that these companies provide can make a difference to an actor who is prepared to be there, they also make money off of the actors who don't know any better. The solution? Actors need to really educate themselves and ask the tough questions before going down this road. Here are the important questions to ask yourself before signing up for these.

Am I ready? This is so important, and where many actors go wrong. Be honest with yourself. Are you in a position in your career where you are ready to be in front of a talent agent or casting director? Many, many actors are not, and are not operating at a competitive level. You have to know your type, your brand, have an amazing headshot, a killer resumé, a great demo reel, and have the money to spend. If you aren't ready, and you keep spending money on these, people will remember you, and if you keep delivering a less than stellar product, it will be harder for you down the road. You should be ready to audition for network TV shows, offer a competitive product, and have the confidence and talent to excel on that higher level.

Have I exhausted every other option? Sometimes sending out mailings isn't enough. Maybe you have sent out tons of headshots, postcards, asked all of your friends for referrals, invited agents to your readings, and emailed your demo reel all over town, to no avail. If the product is good, and they *need* you, they will take notice. Maybe you are frustrated with the student film world, have done so much free work, that you are ready to be auditioning for bigger roles. If you have done everything, and feel like you are hitting a wall, then maybe now is the time to consider doing some targeted "Pay-to Meets."

Agent, manager, or casting director? Commercials or theatrical? If you are ready, then you have to have a plan. Do you want to target certain agents or casting directors? If you are targeting agents, do your research! Research the agents, find out how big they are, what they specialize in, and decide if they are right for you. Maybe you want to target a manager who has fewer clients and can really bring you to the next step. Go on IMDb-Pro, look up their client list, see if they have developmental clients, and if they have anyone already like you. Maybe you have more of a commercial look, and want to target commercial agents. If you are going to target casting directors, make sure they are *actively* casting. That means they are casting right now, on a show that you are right for. I suggest targeting five theatrical agents, five commercial agents, five casting directors (actively casting shows you are right for), and five managers.

What do I expect in the interview? You will have five minutes in the room, and someone will knock on that door when your time is up. Use it wisely. Present a scene that is right for you, and something you could realistically be cast as. Look your best! Short and sweet, at most two pages, with you doing most of the talking. Know three shows that you are right for (ones that are casting in your city, not on the opposite coast). Know your six-month plan and be prepared to summarize it ("I want to book three co-star roles and then move up to guest stars, etc.")

What do I expect from this? A lot of the time, they will just say, "*Great job! Nice to meet you.*" Sometimes they will be very excited about you, tell you to email them the next day, and then you will never hear back. Some will want to start freelancing with you right away, and you will never hear from them. Some will tell you to "let them know when you book something." Some will want to sign you and start getting you auditions immediately. Remember that all of them are being paid to be there, and some aren't necessarily looking for new talent. This is why the websites for these companies say, "These are for educational purposes only, and are not a guarantee of employment." You have to think of it as a chance to start a relationship with someone, for someone to get to know your work, and to not expect anything from it right away.

The bottom line is you have to decide for yourself if you are ready, and if you genuinely feel like this will get you to that next step. Keep working at your craft, keep putting good work out there, and developing relationships.

Don't just sign up and spend tons of money to meet agents because they are big and have a bi-coastal offices and you heard they represent Tobey Maguire. You ain't Tobey. You ain't anybody. Yet. Be smart about where you are in your career, and decide if this kind of agent would be a good fit for you.

The Final Step

An agent or manager can get you that big audition that could change your life. As I said before, there are tons and tons of actors in New York City and Los Angeles. You have to be ready to compete at this level, amongst many other talented actors. Just because you were the lead in your school's musical does not mean you will get representation right away. Just because you are pretty does not mean you will book work. Agents and managers are looking for the total package, and for someone who will make them money. They want actors who are professionals, who show up on time, are prepared, always look their best, are "good in the room," and know exactly how they fit into the marketplace. It's your job to figure that out and develop your skills before you compete at this level, so that you are ready when the perfect audition comes your way.

Avoiding Scams

"WANNA BE FAMOUS??? Come down to the Holiday Inn in Norfolk, Nebraska THIS SATURDAY ONLY and meet one of Hollywood's LEADING casting directors! This could be your chance to become a star! Only $500!!"-every small town radio station

How many times have you heard this on the radio in your hometown? Then you see hundreds of people standing in line outside the hotel with their headshots (that their friend took), hoping that this will be their big break, they will finally get discovered and can quit their supermarket job. Then they will be famous, move to Hollywood, and all will be right in the world. Um...not so much.

S.C.A.M. Someone Capitalizing on Actor's Money.

Here's the deal. If it's too good to be true, it probably is. Getting discovered at a hotel? Doesn't happen. Especially in a small town in the middle of nowhere. There are lots of scams out there (some obvious, some less so), and it's an actor's responsibility to educate themselves on how this business works, so they don't fall victim to it. Read books, blogs, websites, reviews, ask a coach, ask your friends, just don't throw your money down blindly to people who sell themselves as "experts." It's hard enough to make money as an actor, and most of us work side jobs to barely get by, so spend wisely! Do more research than you think is necessary. I've had many clients come to me after having spent *thousands* on these different money-making schemes, only to leave disappointed and frustrated and broke. An expensive cruise in the Caribbean where you get to "mingle with industry veterans?" Come on.

Getting Ripped Off

Ah, the internet. Google is an amazing tool, as you can find out a lot of information about a company, and possibly some reviews from the actors who attended. You can also look at *www.ripoffreport.com*, as that sometimes mentions talent agencies and managers that are known for swindling money. Sometimes they get busted, and change their company name several times, and still take money from actors. Crazy, right? Read contracts thoroughly. As long as there is a huge supply of actors out there, there will be huge supply of people trying to take money from them. As long as there are actors looking to get famous quickly, they will keep spending the money.

No Money Up Front

If an agent asks for money up front, walk away. Agents only make money when you make money. That is the rule. If a website charges you $400 to post all your info online and send you access to auditions, it's a scam. There are a few legitimate audition sites (mentioned earlier). Just stick to those.

The Famous Kickback

If an agency calls you and says they want to work with you, but you need to get new headshots and take classes, and they refer you to "someone they know," more often than not, it's a scam. They know you want an agent, so they are calling you in and then farming out business to their friends, and probably getting a kickback in return. This isn't always the case, but I've heard enough horror stories.

There are many more out there, and specific companies I could name, but I'll end by saying this-- If you are in this to get famous, there is no quick fix. There are far more actors out there than there are jobs, and as long as that supply vs. demand factor remains (which it will), there will *always* be companies popping up trying to take your money. So be smart, patient, trust your gut, and continue putting good work out there. In this business, there are no guarantees. So anyone who *promises* you they will get you work or help you meet "top industry executives" is a scam. This is why all actors have to be savvy, and have business sense. It's not enough to be a good actor. You have to be a smart, educated, businessperson as well. And you have to be able to smell B.S. a mile away.

I think because this business is so difficult, actors are looking to get a leg up in whatever way they can, and will do anything to stand out. It's a cutthroat business, so any and all information is deemed "useful." But honestly, it really comes down to persistence, training, luck and timing, and you really can't control the rest.

Be smart. Be careful. Do your research. There is no quick way to break in.

Survival Jobs

It seems this question comes up every single day from one of my students: "How do I make money while still being available for auditions? Do I have to wait tables?" The answer is, you don't. Having been a professional actor for fifteen years, I've done everything from temp work, to serving food to dolls, dog walking, and even working the graveyard shift at a physical therapy office. Working at a bar or restaurant is not for everyone. While the money can be good, it can also keep you up late, leaving you tired and not at your best at auditions.

Unless you can find that dream full-time job with salary and benefits that allows you the chance to pursue acting, you have to be smart, resourceful, and flexible to create a steady income flow until you book that first national commercial, or that first guest-starring role. What other skills do you have? Is there a job (or two or three) you can do that makes you happy (or at least that you can tolerate) *while* you are pursuing your dream? To achieve this might mean some creative thinking.

Temp Work. If you are good with computers and can type fast, this is great. I did this for the first two years I lived in New York and loved it. You work in an office environment (with very little responsibility), can make from $12-$20/hour, and you have your nights free. When auditions come up, you either leave your temp job for an hour or call out for the day. You can take jobs that are day-to-day, or week-to-week, and do theatre at night, plus you work the same hours as most of your friends, allowing you to carve out a social life. There are tons of temp agencies in New York and Los Angeles, and some even specialize in entertainment jobs.

Personal Trainer. If you are physically fit, work out, and are interested in health and nutrition, this is a great option (with very flexible hours). You decide how hard you work, how many clients you have, and how much money you make. You can become certified as a low-level trainer by doing a basic two-day seminar. Some gyms even offer free membership to trainers as well.

Dog Walker. I did this for a year in Los Angeles. If you love dogs and being outside, this is a great option. Early morning, late evening, and weekend hours make it very easy to balance with auditions. You can freelance by putting up flyers and handing out business cards, or you can work for a staffing company (sort of like a temp agency) that will take a cut of the fee and give you lots of opportunities.

Nanny/Babysitter. Great gig, and potentially very lucrative if you are good with kids. You can work on your sides while they sleep. (Or if you're lucky, they can run lines with you!)

Promo Work/Modeling. You can find these jobs on Craigslist, or sign up with a promo company. They put out a "breakdown," you send them your headshot, and they "cast" you. You might spend the day handing out flyers in Times Square, or hosting a cocktail event at a restaurant.

Personal Assistant. I know a lot of actors who do this, and find it very rewarding— if you are willing to set ego aside and be prepared to do someone else's chores.

Real Estate Broker. Get your license and start looking to match potential renters with landlords. It's a tough market, and you work on commission, but if you get your foot in the door, this can be a great side gig.

Catering. You've seen *Party Down*, right? Paid by the hour, plus tips. Different location every time.

Tutoring. You can freelance or work for a staffing company, and they will match you up with parents looking for private tutors in specific subjects. Maybe that geometry class will come in handy after all.

Video Editor. Your friends are actors, right? Help them with their demo reels! If you have a Mac, go take a free iMovie seminar at the Apple store, and become a master video editor. It will come in handy for the rest of your career, and someone always needs footage edited.

Bartending/Server/Host. Yes, this is an obvious one, but there's a reason. You work nights and weekends (leaving your days open for auditions), and you make quick money. I wore a pink apron and served dolls once. Big money, folks.

Yoga/Pilates Teacher. If you can get your certification, this is a great, flexible way to make money.

Airbnb. Rent out your apartment to strangers. Yay!

Web Design. Become an expert at this, and you will be doing you friends' actor websites for years to come.

It's all about finding what works for you, what makes you happy, and what you are willing to put up with while you pursue your dream. Until you land your first big job (and maybe even after), it's about living paycheck to paycheck, day to day, scrambling around from job to job, memorizing lines, racing to student film auditions, looking for agents, doing free theatre, and living a "freelance" lifestyle, making yourself available and ready for when that big opportunity presents itself.

Kids and Teens

Everyone's kid is "adorable." Let's agree on that. But when does that become "Let's see if we can make a career out of this." When is the right time to move to New York or Los Angeles? When is it time to "go pro?" It all depends on where you are at with your son or daughter's career. If you don't live in a major market and are just starting out, then the best advice I could ever give is to get involved with any and all community theatre in your hometown. This kind of experience is wonderful for a young kid or teen actor, where they learn to create characters in a fun environment, with other actors their age, and there isn't that added pressure of "booking the job." When I was in middle school, I started doing lots of theatre, which helped break me out of my shell and develop my confidence (both as an actor and as a person), which made me want to continue as I went into high school, college, and then after college. Young actors have wonderful imaginations, and the more they tap into that, the better actor they will be. Work on building up their resumés, finding the joy in playing these interesting characters, and most importantly, make sure it is fun for them.

Going Pro

The time to "go pro" and make the move to New York or Los Angeles is when your young actor has been discovered by an agent or manager, and is interested in aggressively sending them out for auditions. I don't mean just self-tapes, I mean they are pitching them and getting them directly in front of the casting director. At this point the young actor is up for big union jobs, there is intense competition, and could potentially make tons of money for landing the gig. They need to learn audition etiquette, how to act on-camera, and what is expected of them. The sacrifice here is that you will be racing around from school, to last minute auditions, callbacks, and it will make your life nuts if you are working a steady 9 to 5 job. It's all about sacrifice. If you are a parent with 3 kids in the business, and they are being sent out for voiceovers, commercials, TV, film, and theatre auditions, then it makes sense for you to be as close as possible to where all the action is. At this point they are being considered for lead roles on TV shows and films, and sometimes these appointments come in the night before. Be careful what you wish for! It's hard to have a life outside of this.

Training

Be careful of too much training at a young age. The number one thing that all casting directors want in on-camera auditions is for kids to act natural, to bring their authentic personality to the audition, to be fully prepared, and to have fun. Kids can be wonderful actors, and tap into extreme emotions at the drop of a hat. They can also be taught bad habits, which can get in the way of delivering a strong audition. Casting directors don't want a young actor to be over-coached or trained when they walk into a room, as it can strip away their natural, completely unselfconscious joy. They want them to be unaffected and full of personality, and totally be themselves in front of a group of strangers in an audition. The wrong class can turn a young actor into a robot, where they are thinking too much, "acting," and not being present in their work. A good teacher will give them the freedom to play, and teach them that there are many different ways of saying a line, but not to "over-rehearse" to the point where they aren't listening anymore.

Headshots

When it comes to kids and teens, it's not important to spend as much money on a headshot at first, because they are still growing, and you would have to get a new headshot every year to keep up. Instead, most agents and casting directors suggest using a simple, high quality, well-lit photo, as long as it shows their personality. Once they stop growing, then step it up and get a really professional picture. One close shot and one three quarters shot is all they need.

Juggling School and Life

OK, moms and dads. This is both a love letter and a cautionary tale. I know how hard you work. You want your kids to do well. You work hard going over the sides, read the scripts for them, take them out of school, rearrange their schedules, and race around from audition to audition, not to mention taking them to their vocal coach, acting coach, dance lessons, school play rehearsal, sports, and everything else they have going on. You are a super parent, and you would do anything to make your kid happy.

There isn't enough time in the day to do everything. At the drop of a hat, you may be asked to fly to the other coast, go on tour with a musical because someone just dropped out, or get ten pages of sides for a last minute callback. It is beyond impressive how much you support your children. It's easy for your kid to feel pressure when they see how stressed you are. At the end of the day, it's all about your kid being relaxed and comfortable when they walk into that room, and then completely letting it go once that audition is over. If they feel that the audition is "very important," their nerves will get in the way. I've seen it happen too many times. Just make sure they are well rested and well prepared for every audition they walk into.

Getting an Agent or Manager

If you are seeking representation, sending in a simple headshot and a nice typed cover letter is all you need to do. Keep it simple, and keep it short. You don't want to just move to New York or L.A. without some kind of representation. Youth agents handle kids and teens up to a certain age (sometimes 25 or 30), and then at that point they can transfer to the adult division. They are less concerned with formal training at the beginning, and far more concerned with presence, likeability, being natural on-camera (and still), and the young actor being professional and well-prepared for their auditions. There are wonderful agents and managers out there for young actors, depending on how big you want to go. Some managers help Broadway actors transition into TV and film, and have the right connections to do so. Nickelodeon and Disney offer lots of opportunities for young actors, and most of those shows film in Los Angeles. If you are in New York, you will most often "go on tape" for the casting directors in Los Angeles, and if you are right for it, they will fly you out for a screen test (exciting).

The Agent-Parent Relationship

If you already have representation and are getting sent out—congratulations. You are in the club, and one of the lucky ones. Agents are so busy during the day, aggressively pitching your son or daughter for every job that comes out on the breakdowns. I'm going to give you some wise advice. Don't call or email them too much about little things, as it keeps them from doing their job. I mean asking for feedback, what shirt to wear, which headshot to use, headband or no headband, etc. If they represent fifty young actors, that's fifty moms or dads calling them on any given day, let's say for at least ten minutes each (500 minutes=Over seven hours!). That's almost a full day of *not* pitching their clients for jobs (which is what you want). That being said, if your young actor gets rejected from a job after getting three callbacks, then ask for feedback. It's your right. Just don't do it for every commercial and TV pre-read. And if your son or daughter is being sent out all the time, and just hasn't gotten any response, then by all means have a discussion with your manager or agent. That's what they are there for.

Audition Preparation

At the end of the day, everyone just wants your kid to book the job. You, your agent, your manager, and the casting director are working their butts off to make that happen. They are giving you a coveted time slot and want the actor to come in and nail it. Nothing else matters—the excuses, the amount of homework they have, the apologies, the drama. Here are some general rules for parents when you get those last minute auditions.

Memorize, memorize, memorize. I know you get the script the night before, and sometimes you get more than one audition for the next day with lots and lots of lines. It's a crazy business, and everything happens very last minute. Most kids aren't prepared enough when they walk into a room, and end up staring down at the script the whole time. Or even worse, instead of listening in the scene, they are just thinking of their next line. It shows in their eyes. The single best thing you can do as a parent is help them memorize their lines. Make it fun. Talk about what the lines mean, and why they would be saying it. Have them try it tons of different ways. You want to make sure they are as prepared as possible so they can go in and be fully present in the scene, and also be open to direction. Just run through the lines, don't coach them.

Read the whole script. Who has the time, right? I'm telling you, it's that important. It should be part of their homework. This is one that not a lot of parents do, but it will give you a huge advantage in auditions, as well as a context for the scenes. Find the time to at least skim through it so you understand what is happening. Many times in a callback situation, the director will ask your kid about the script, the character, and the circumstances. You want them to be prepared for this. There are clues in the script that will help fuel the scene. Read the crossed out lines right before the scene starts and dig for clues about the character.

Don't obsess about the breakdowns. If the character description calls for a "precocious, whimsical, happy go lucky nine year old" don't worry about *forcing* your kid to act that way in the scene. It will be there or it won't. Breakdowns are just a guide, and often times they change. With everyone reading the same lines, it's the personality that stands out--the wonderful, original, authentic essence of that actor. That is why they are cast. Of course you want to *suggest* the character, but the second you try too hard it becomes a red flag and looks forced in the audition.

Don't worry about the clothing and hair too much. This isn't *Toddlers & Tiaras.* Of course it's important to dress *like* the character, but you never want it to be a costume. If you worry too much about the color of the shirt, and whether or not the hair should be parted in the middle or off to the side, you are going in the wrong direction. Nobody ever lost a part because their shirt was blue instead of red. It's about the essence of the person, and how they come across on camera. Too much costume can make it seem like they are overcompensating for their acting skills.

Leave the coaching to the pros. I have to be honest here. I know you want them to do well, but sometimes your coaching gets in the way. Avoid line readings, planned gestures and facial expressions, and trying to "give them what they are looking for." Many times this makes a casting director's job so much harder as they try to find the real person underneath all the unnatural "acting" stuff. A good coach will help them free up the lines and make it spontaneous, while also finding the right emotion and tone for the script and how to give the character a strong inner life. Forced line readings create a very stiff, overly rehearsed performance and a casting director can spot that a mile away.

It's okay to say "no." You were just given three auditions for tomorrow, as well as a self-tape. It's too much! It is far better to have two auditions that are fully prepared for, than four mediocre auditions. Pick and choose the ones you feel are most important, and pass on the others. You don't want your kid to get burnt out. Your agent won't be mad, I promise.

Master on-camera audition etiquette. Just be natural and listen. That's all any casting director wants. Most kids who come from the stage end up projecting too much, exaggerating their facial expressions, and not paying attention to the intimacy and stillness of an on-camera environment. It's the easiest way to make sure they *don't* get the job. They should walk into the room with confidence (naturally), learn to slate their name into the camera (naturally), take a breath, and then disappear into the scene (naturally). The more rested they are and the more focus they have, the less fidgety they are. The last thing you want is for your kid to show up to an audition yawning, moving around in the chair, and completely distracted. On-camera auditions are about concentration, stillness, and listening. They should sit up in the chair (or stand), look at the reader off-camera, and focus their eyes on that person. Never look into camera (unless it's a slate), and avoid the eyes wandering around too much.

Manage their expectations. There is absolutely no need to tell your kid that this is "an important audition." It should be fun, just another chance for them to play. Most of the time it comes down to whether or not they are the right height, or have the right color hair. It's out of your hands! Do the work, show up on time, and then let it go. The more you talk about how big the audition is, the more nervous you make them. It only keeps them from doing their best, and stresses them out. They should be fully relaxed in the audition so they can let their imaginations run wild. Once the audition is done, move on. There are always more auditions around the corner.

Once they book the job, you have to know what to expect. There are far too many laws to go over here, but check out the wonderful advice at Biz Parents Foundation (www.bizparentz.org). It will help you navigate the business side of this career.

New York vs. Los Angeles

Interview with Matt and Becki Newton

Do you prefer being an actor in New York or L.A?

Matt: I'm an East Coast guy, so I love New York. You can walk to all of your auditions. There aren't nearly as many casting directors here, so if they all like you, they bring you in for everything. L.A. was beautiful and all, but I always felt like everyone out there was an actor, and it didn't seem like they took training as seriously. Also, it can be a bit lonely, as it's so spread out and you spend so much time in your car.

Becki: I started out a die-hard New Yorker, but really grew to love working in Los Angeles. Even though I originally wanted to do theater, TV presented more opportunities for me, which led me out west. Eventually I came to appreciate the car culture as well as it pertained to auditioning. I would rather sit in traffic listening to the radio en route to a meeting than freeze my butt off hailing a cab to Chelsea Piers. So what started as more opportunity led to greater comfort due to the climate.

Are there more opportunities for actors in New York or L.A.?

Matt: It's hard so say. I moved to New York after graduating from Vassar, and six months later I moved to L.A., because at the time there was way more happening there in the film and TV market (and I had a bicoastal agent who suggested I test the waters out there). Now, New York has now become a very important TV market, with over thirty shows filming here and counting. It's a great time to be an actor here, and actors can build up a bunch of credits (co-stars, guest stars, etc.). However, there aren't a lot of sitcoms here, so if that's your thing, go to L.A. If you are a theater actor, I think New York has more opportunities. A lot of film production is moving out of Los Angeles to cities like Austin and Atlanta.

Becki: There are tons of opportunities in both places. Commercially, I found equal opportunities on both coasts. The obvious difference is theater, which I believe one must be in NYC to train and pursue seriously.

What is pilot season like in L.A. vs. New York?

Matt: For the most part, actors go "on tape" in New York for the bigger series regular roles in pilots that are filming out of L.A., which means they upload the audition and the producers in L.A. can watch it the same day. You could have five auditions a day, walk around to the different studios, and that night hear that you are flying out to L.A. for a screen test. When I lived in L.A., you could go in for a producer's session, and then screen test later that day. Everything is last minute and crazy. It can get a bit nutty out there. Now that Netflix and Amazon are offering original programming, pilot season is more year-round.

Becki: I booked 'Ugly Betty' while visiting L.A. for pilot season. I found more momentum in L.A. There was also an element of no one knowing me in L.A. that I liked. In NYC, I auditioned for mostly "quirky friend" roles. Since casting directors in L.A. lacked a preconceived notion of me, I was able to reinvent my type a bit, which was essential in booking the role of Amanda on 'Ugly Betty.' I don't believe I would have auditioned for that role in N.Y.

What advice would you give an actor new to the business?

Matt: Move to the city that makes you the most comfortable, where you have a good support system. Create your own work, self-produce, take classes, network, and work as hard as you can. There are so many actors trying to do this, so you have to zero in on what sets you apart, really hone your skills, figure out your type and your place in the market, and target your buyers—maybe that involves doing staged readings in New York, or producing your own YouTube videos in L.A.

Becki: I would say to an actor new to the business that it's best to go where you are most comfortable as a person, both in and outside of the business. My brother had already spent time in L.A. as a working actor, and my husband, actor Chris Diamantopoulos, would often travel with me, since he was ready to explore the West Coast as well. So I had a mini network built in, which helped me endure the ups and downs more easily. I would not have felt comfortable coming out to L.A. without Matt and Chris.

How did you find your agent?

Matt: I had sent out my headshots to over fifty agents in New York, and done lots of in person drop-offs, and several of them started freelancing with me. In New York all the agents are in the same seven buildings, so it's easier to take a few hours and slide some pictures under the door. Then I booked a role on 'Strangers with Candy,' which is when I decided to sign with one.

Becki: I found my agent in L.A. through my N.Y. agent. They had an office on both coasts and were very supportive of actors spending time in L.A. I found my N.Y. agent after blindly mailing out about five hundred headshots.

Do you think it's smart to do extra work?

Matt: I did one day on 'Guiding Light' after doing a Shakespeare monologue for the under five casting director. I hated it, and decided never to do it again. I think it's good to do it once to see what it's like on a set, learn the lingo, and understand the pacing of it, but don't make a habit of it.

Becki: I think extra work is helpful to people who've never experienced working on a set. I had worked in commercials before television, which helped me immensely when I showed up on set for my first TV job ('Law and Order SVU'). On 'Ugly Betty,' I saw many instances where extras were given opportunities to audition for bigger roles on the show.

How important is training?

Matt: I think training is important, as long as you don't develop any bad habits. I think seeing yourself on camera, and learning how to act and how to audition is an essential part of the business. I also think "on the job training" can sometimes be better than any acting class (if you are lucky enough to book the job).

Becki: Training is hugely important wherever you decide to audition and work. I would love to pursue theater more seriously someday, and know that my technique would need a lot of work before I made that step. I have a degree in European history, which didn't necessarily have any direct impact on my career, but I'm grateful I studied something other than acting in college.

Mostly I've had on-the-job training for on camera work. The commercials were so helpful in simply being comfortable on camera and on sets. And when I was lucky enough to get the 'Ugly Betty' job, I had some of the best actors around to guide me. It was probably the greatest master class I could have asked for.

The Realities of Being on Set

"Hurry up and wait."

Your first TV role. It's nerve-wracking. Everything you have trained for has been leading up to this moment. You get your call time, show up (after not much sleep), wait for hours sitting in your tiny trailer obsessing over your three lines waiting for them to call you. You are about to fall asleep, when the second A.D. finally knocks on your door and says, *"We are ready for you!"* and walks you to the location.

Most actors have no idea what to expect when they walk onto a huge TV set for the first time. This isn't a student film. There are dozens of people on the crew, and they already know each other. They are like a family, where everyone has a very specific job to help make you look good.

Everyone expects you to know what you are doing. But the truth is, you have absolutely no idea. Nothing prepares you for the reality of being on a real set for the first time. There are so many things going on that it's hard to focus on your acting. So how do you prepare yourself mentally? Here is what you need to know

You will probably only get one rehearsal. "What? But when I did 'Grease' in college I had *fifteen weeks* of rehearsal." Not anymore. If this is a one-hour drama or a single-camera comedy, you will most likely get one tiny little rehearsal, and you will be working with people you have never met before. You will say a brief hello to the director (who you probably saw at the callback), and who is extremely busy, and then you will run through the lines with the other actors at the location. They will discuss the blocking, talk briefly about the scene, and then do a "marking rehearsal," where the crew comes in and they figure out where everyone will be standing so they can set up the lights. That's right, dozens of eyes on you. Be confident and act like you have been doing this forever.

Know your lines. Backwards and forwards. Inside and out. Nobody else will (which will be confusing to you, as they are getting paid so much more than you), but you must, as you are the guest, and you won this job over many, many actors. You can be replaced easily. They might change your lines, they might cut

92

them. Be ready for anything, and don't take it personally. There will be so many distractions on set (elaborate camera moves, trying to hit your mark, finding your light), and if you aren't secure with the lines, you will waste valuable time (and light, and money). You will probably get one or two takes of your shot. If you mess up a line,the script supervisor will shout out your line for you. They are your new best friend.

Don't change anything! When you show up on set, do exactly what you did in the audition and the callback, but be very open to direction. Don't overthink it, and please don't meet with a coach *after* you booked the job and suddenly make big changes to your character. It's a "one and done" role, and you are there to serve the story, and that is your job. If your line is "More water for you, sir?" don't come up with a detailed backstory about how you just found out your best friend died of cancer and suddenly decide you should be crying in your scene.

It's not about you. Four years of drama school? Nobody cares. Won the audience award at your hometown "film festival" for your performance as Stanley Kowalski in an updated *Streetcar* musical? Doesn't matter. You are one of many small characters here to fill the world of this TV show. It's about the series regulars, their storylines, and you are there as a peripheral character. As Harold Guskin said, "Don't make a meal out of a snack." Know your place in the hierarchy, be a total professional, don't complain, and don't overthink your lines. Nobody cares about your character's backstory, or why Momma didn't pay attention to you growing up. Don't expect a standing ovation when you finish. Most of the crew are ready to go home and go to sleep. No feedback is good feedback.

Look over your contract. In the chaos of a film set, actors hurriedly sign the contracts in their dressing rooms, assuming it's right. I promise you, half the time it's not. Look it over, make sure it's what you and your agent agreed on in terms of rate and billing.

Hit your marks. If you don't, you will be out of focus. It's that simple. They put colored tape marks on the ground so they can focus the camera on that particular spot. You want to be in focus when you get your big close-up, right? You are expected to hit that mark without looking at it. This takes skill.

Know the shots. Pay attention to your frame. If it's a close-up, don't be a flailing chicken in your acting. If it's a master shot, flail all you want. The other shots you need to know are "over the shoulder," "handheld," "two shot," "medium close-up," and "tight close-up." Learn them. Master them. Knowing your frame will allow you to calibrate your performance accordingly and give the editor some great footage to choose from, and therefore better footage for your reel.

Don't complain. Say thank you to everybody. You're tired, I get it. You've been waiting six hours to get to your scene. Don't. Ever. Complain. You are so lucky to be there. Remember, everyone's been there longer than you, especially the makeup artists. When you wrap, say thank you to everyone, especially the writer and director. They will work on other projects, and will remember your professionalism. They will also remember if you were a total diva and ruined everyone's day. Send a "thank you" card to the casting director. They are the ones who brought you in in the first place.

"Room tone" means shut up. I learned this the hard way. There's a little button on the side of your phone that turns it to silent. Don't be that guy.

10 Questions For a Casting Director

Kimberly Graham is the Associate Casting Director for Showtime's Emmy Award winner *Homeland*

What's the biggest piece of advice you would give for an actor breaking into the business?

Kim: Learn how to manage your time. If you are serious about becoming an actor, you have to take care of yourself and work on your craft daily. I see too many young people come out of college, move to NYC, get a job and then the craft isn't maintained. If you are not in a class, you should be reading plays, watching television, seeing films. This should be your full time job.

How does a newer actor go about getting seen by a major casting director?

Kim: Networking is key, especially when you don't have representation. There are many companies in the city that provide workshops and classes taught by industry that are invaluable to both parties. It gives us a chance to meet new talent we wouldn't otherwise have an opportunity to, and it gives the talent an opportunity to show their stuff.

What are the dos and don'ts in an audition?

Kim: Let me try a positive spin on this. Those 5 minutes in the room is your time. Use it wisely. Be gracious and listen to direction. Show us WHO the character is. When dismissed, say thank you and leave. Best audition ever!!

Are meet and greet workshops worth it?

Kim: There are so many actors to remember and new ones I haven't met so I do find them valuable. It's good to keep yourself on my radar.

How important is it for actors to know their type and have their headshot reflect that?

Kim: *Knowing your type is key and reflecting that in your headshot as well as in the work. A lot of actors try to sell what they WANT to be, and not who they ARE. Embrace all that is you and sell it. No one is going to do what you do.*

How many submissions do you get for 1 line on a TV show?

Kim: *I've gotten up to over 2,000 for one role. Crazy, eh?*

What makes a good demo reel?

Kim: *It should be short (under two minutes) and should have your best stuff first. That student film you did, that was well shot, is more valuable if there is good footage than the one line you had on 'Law and Order'. Put that first. And make sure you invest in a good editor. It can make or break whether or not someone will bring you in. Better to have no reel than one that is done poorly.*

How important is training?

Kim: *You might be able to get away with little training in film/TV but definitely not in theater. However, I do believe training is key. Where and who you study with tells me a lot about the kind of actor I expect.*

What's the main difference between auditioning for tv and theatre?

Kim: *For me, the performance is a matter of scale. Your playing space is different. Theatre is about words and projection. TV is a visual medium. The camera comes into your world, you don't go out to it.*

How much control do actors have over getting cast?

Kim: *None. There are so many factors involved in casting, so many opinions and much strategy in creating a piece of work. The only control they have is what they do in the room. Actors need to learn what they have control over, what they don't and knowing the difference.*

In Closing

Let's be real for a moment. Sometimes this business gets incredibly frustrating, and it's easy to get down on yourself with all of the rejection that comes along with deciding to pursue acting as a career. You keep getting knocked down, and sometimes it gets harder and harder to keep getting back up and dusting yourself off. Sometimes it feels like everyone else is getting their big break, and you aren't. You wonder if your turn will ever come. It's not easy to break into acting.

Sure, you'll hear stories of people booking a big TV job on their very first audition. You'll hear about how actors were discovered on the street, or by accident, and put in a movie. Chris Klein (*American Pie*) was discovered while the director was walking through his high school in Nebraska. For all of those stories, there are tons more of well known actors getting fired from pilots, cut out of movies, or not getting their big break until they were well into their forties or later. There are actors who have worked steadily for their entire lives, and most people have never heard of them. These actors are *talented,* and even though one project didn't work out, they kept working on their craft, auditioning well, and putting good work out there. They developed a *reputation* for being good, and for being professional, and being someone people wanted to work with.

There's always that relative at the Thanksgiving table who is going to toss out the infamous, *"When am I going to see you on TV?"* or *"When are you going to get a real job?"*— adding embarrassment to the stress you are already feeling. Jenna Fischer wrote an amazing article on the actor's struggle after she booked her role as Pam on *The Office,* and how long it took for her to get that job and how difficult it was. Nobody truly understands what it means to get the callback, and how "booking the room" is just as good as booking the job, and how exciting it is to land a role in your first student film.

Maybe you have spent months submitting to tons of projects, on all the casting websites, and you simply aren't getting called in. Your monologues are getting rusty. Or maybe you are auditioning all the time, but nobody wants to hire you. Or spending hundreds (or thousands) on pay-to-meet workshops and not getting any bites from agents or casting directors. You start to question everything from your headshot, to your talent, to your financial situation, to your life choices. You probably have thought about quitting many times.

Here's the deal: It is difficult to have a career in acting. It's a freelance job that involves a lot of unpaid work and hard hours, leaving your survival job at the drop of a hat, with very little return on investment. People think we are crazy for doing it. It is a constant sacrifice, and you're constantly worrying where your next paycheck is coming from. Some people work so hard at it for many years and it never pays off. Some people get their lucky break right away, without any formal training. It's a constant battle, and sometimes there is no rhyme or reason why some make it, and some don't.

So why do we do it? We do it because it makes us happy, it drives us, and it gives us the freedom to explore ourselves, on camera and on stage, in different characters, to have fun with like-minded people, to let go and not worry about the consequences. There's nothing better than walking on stage for the first time and having the audience respond to you, or the first time you hit your mark and say a line on set. It is fulfilling in ways that other "non-creatives" simply don't understand. Some people choose to give up their secure corporate jobs with a 401k and amazing benefits simply for the chance to be actors, to express themselves creatively, whether in a classroom or on a set. These are people that just want to live a more exciting life, regardless of the outcome. For most actors, it's simply not about money, which is hard for others to understand.

I cried the first time I got an acting gig on a TV show. That's how badly I wanted it. It was the first time I could show my family that my hard work was paying off. The confused look on my mom's face while watching Amy Sedaris act like a high school girl on *Strangers with Candy* was priceless.

Most of time we remind ourselves of that old adage: "If you can do anything else besides acting, then do it." It implies that we don't have our hearts in it, that we aren't fully committed, and therefore, won't succeed. I disagree. I think that the best actors are the ones that have many interests and many different skills, are well-rounded, and think of acting simply as a wonderful hobby, like a sport. If they make money, great. If not, they have other things that make them happy, other skills, other interests, other lives outside of acting. If nothing else, it takes the pressure off, and allows us to feel free and open to wherever this career takes us. They relish in the struggle of it, instead of backing away from it.

The next time you are feeling frustrated, remind yourself why you are doing this. If you are spending all of your time auditioning, and no time in class or on set, then you need to change that so you are creatively fulfilled, and really working on material in-depth, strengthening your creative muscles, working with other actors who love it as much as you do. Don't do it for the fame, or for the money, because you will be sorely disappointed.

This is a wonderful career, and nobody is forcing you to do it. Write down what you are getting out of it, so you can see it in front of you. In plain words. Put it up on your mirror and remind yourself every day. You are so lucky to be able to pursue this amazing journey.

Good luck!
Matt

Appendix A

CASTING WEBSITES
Backstage (www.backstage.com)
Actors Access (www.actorsaccess.com)
Casting Networks (www.castingnetworks.com)
NY Castings (www.nycastings.com)
Mandy (www.Mandy.com)

RESEARCH WEBSITES
IMDb-Pro (www.pro.imdb.com)
Casting About (www.castingabout.com)
Deadline Hollywood (www.deadlinehollywood.com)
Variety (www.variety.com)

UNIONS
SAG-AFTRA (www.sagaftra.org)
ACTORS' EQUITY (www.actorsequity.org)

INFO FOR KIDS AND TEENS
BizParentz Foundation (http://www.bizparentz.org)

RECOMMENDED READING
The Present Actor by Marci Phillips
How to Get the Part Without Falling Apart by Margi Haber
The Charisma Myth by Olivia Fox Cabane
Acting as a Business by Brian O'Neill
Self Management for Actors by Bonnie Gillespie
How to Stop Acting by Harold Guskin
Respect for Acting by Uta Hagen
The Art of Acting by Stella Adler
An Actor Prepares by Stanislavsky
On Acting by Sanford Meisner

Appendix B

Sample resumé

MATT NEWTON

SAG-AFTRA
Cell phone
Email
www.MattNewton.com

Height: 5'8"
Weight: 145
Eyes: Blue
Hair: Brown

THEATRE

Guys and Dolls	Sky Masterson	Guilford High School
Oliver	Artful Dodger	Coal Bin Theatre/Vassar College

FILM

The Road to Glory	Lead	NYU/Dir. Tim Smith
Van Wilder	Principle	Dir. Walt Becker/New Line

TV

The Frenchie (webseries)	Recurring	Dir. Tim Smith
Blue Bloods	Costar	CBS

TRAINING

Vassar College (BA in Drama)		
Audition Workshop	MN Acting Studio	NYC

SKILLS

Soccer, guitar, improve, belt to high C, military weapons, speak Hebrew, Spanish

About the Author

Matt is the founder of the acclaimed MN Acting Studio in New York City, the on-set coach for the hit CBS show *Blue Bloods,* and is a contributing industry expert for the highly prestigious *Backstage.* Matt has coached Emmy Award winners, Golden Globe nominees, and his students have appeared on countless TV shows and films. In addition to his private coaching, Skype, and on-camera classes, Matt also teaches workshops to actors and business professionals all over the world.

Matt has guest starred on countless TV shows, including *Strangers with Candy, Royal Pains, The Americans, Ugly Betty, Dragnet, Miracles, Judging Amy, J.A.G., Guiding Light, As the World Turns, Criminal Minds, Drake and Josh Go Hollywood, and Gilmore Girls.* He has appeared in many films, including *Men Who Stare at Goats* (with Jeff Bridges), *Van Wilder* (with Ryan Reynolds), *Dahmer* (with Jeremy Renner), and the lead role in *Poster Boy* (with Karen Allen), for which he received rave reviews. He also won Best Actor at the Philadelphia First Glance Film Festival for his role in the film *Peace of Mind.*

Matt earned a degree in Drama from Vassar College, where he studied acting under Erin Mee (daughter of Charles Mee) and Dennis Reid. He also studied at the highly regarded National Theatre Institute in Waterford, CT (where he is also on the faculty). After college, he trained with acclaimed teacher Arthur Mendoza at the Actor's Circle Theatre in Los Angeles.

Matt currently lives in New York City with his wife and their two French bulldogs. He is a member of SAG-AFTRA, and is represented by Leading Artists Agency. His sister, Becki Newton, lives in Los Angeles, and is well known for her turn as Amanda on *Ugly Betty* and *How I Met Your Mother.*

To learn more about Matt's classes and coaching, visit www.MNActingStudio.com.

Made in the USA
Middletown, DE
27 October 2015